CONCORDIA UNIVERSITY

D756.5.N6T8
INVASION 44 1ST AMERICAN ED NEW

3 4211 000021049

W9-ACO-309

WITHDRAWN

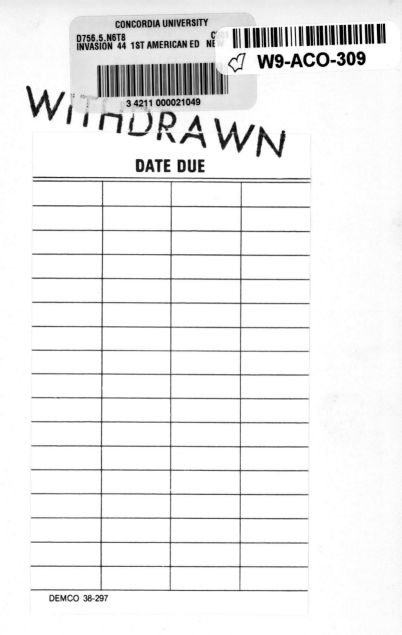

DATE DUE

DEMCO 38-297

INVASION '44

Library
Concordia Teachers College
River Forest, Illinois

INVASION '44

The first full story of D-Day in Normandy

JOHN FRAYN TURNER

G. P. Putnam's Sons   NEW YORK

© 1959 BY JOHN FRAYN TURNER

First American Edition

*All rights reserved. This book, or parts thereof, must
not be reproduced in any form without permission.*

Library of Congress Catalog
Card Number: 59-9756

MANUFACTURED IN THE UNITED STATES OF AMERICA

VAN REES PRESS • NEW YORK

53391

Acknowledgments

I AM sincerely grateful for permission to refer to the following: *The Struggle for Europe* by Chester Wilmot (Harper & Brothers), *The Last Passage* by J. E. Taylor (George Allen and Unwin), *The Red Beret* by Hilary St. George Saunders (Michael Joseph), *The Frogmen* by T. J. Waldron and James Gleeson (Evans Bros.), *Midget Raiders* (*Above Us the Waves*) by C. E. T. Warren and James Benson (Sloane Associates), *The Marines Were There* by Sir Robert Bruce Lockhart (Putnam), and "This Was D-Day" by Cliff Bowering (*The Legionary,* National Magazine of the Canadian Legion).

In addition to these, my bibliography includes *Omaha Beachhead* (United States War Department, Historical Division), *Utah Beach to Cherbourg* (United States War Department, Historical Division), *The Second World War,* Volume V, *Closing the Ring,* by Winston S. Churchill (Houghton Mifflin), *Crusade in Europe* by Dwight D. Eisenhower (Doubleday), *Normandy to the Baltic* by Field Marshal the Viscount Montgomery of Alamein (Hutchinson), *The Secret War* by Gerald Pawle (Sloane Associates), *Service Most Silent* by John Frayn Turner (British Book Centre), *Invasion* by John St. John Cooper (Daily Express Publications), "The Assault Phase of the Normandy Landings" (London *Gazette*), "Air Operations by the Allied Expeditionary Air Force in North-West Europe" (London *Gazette*).

5

Photographic illustrations will be found following page 96.

INVASION '44

One

As the great German juggernaut thundered through the Low Countries in mid-May, 1940, within a week the British Expeditionary Force was in drastic danger. An emergency meeting at the War Office on May 19 considered as a temporary measure maintaining it through Dunkirk, Calais and Boulogne, and as an alarming alternative, partial or total evacuation via the same three places. The need for evacuation was still thought "to be unlikely." Whether the British Expeditionary Force was to stay or leave, however, naval command was to be controlled direct from Dover by Admiral Bertram Ramsay.

During the next two days, conditions on the Continent grew worse each hour, and on May 21 the British War Office were considering "emergency evacuation" of very large forces. So throughout the week the now immortal small ships and still smaller boats assembled around the Kent coast, while over in Belgium four divisions of the B.E.F. were in imminent danger of encirclement near Lille.

Then at 10 P.M. on Sunday, May 26, exactly one week after the War Office had thought evacuation unlikely, Ramsay received the order to implement Operation Dynamo. The most expected from this was to save 45,000 men in the estimated two days left before the enemy would reach the coast. One man in eight of the B.E.F.

But for some reason, the German tanks headed away from the retreating British troops, giving them an extra week before the all-out attack.

The result was Dunkirk.

At this moment of memorable defeat, two men typified the will

9

to win, which was expressed four years later on the day of deliverance. Their names: Bertram Ramsay and Charles Goodeve. How right that Ramsay, the savior of the B.E.F., should carry the Allies back into France on D-Day. And how amazing that in the midst of the struggle for survival during those last days of May, 1940, Charles Goodeve should go down to Dover to try and find himself a job in which he could help win the war.

Lieutenant Commander Goodeve, R.N.V.R., a brilliant scientist, heard of a new weapons department the Admiralty were setting up under a Vice-Admiral Somerville. He tried to telephone the Admiral but was told that Somerville was at Dover helping Ramsay, who had been working right round the clock without relief.

Not knowing exactly what was happening at Dover, Goodeve decided to risk a visit and caught a train for Dover the same night. In Ramsay's house above the fortress at Dover, Goodeve met Somerville and heard from him how Allied shipping was desperately short of close-range weapons to combat the German air offensive. Somerville foresaw how bomber attacks on our ships could strangle war supplies. Here then was the next stage in the battle: too soon to talk of attack. But back in the Dynamo operations room, where Somerville relieved Ramsay at 2:30 A.M. each morning, they did talk of many possible projects for ultimate victory and it was dawn when Goodeve walked down the hill to catch the first train to London. Ships were bringing men back from Dunkirk—the living and the dead. In the train, too, were more men from France, sleeping for the first time in a week or more. Goodeve carried in his pocket a request from Somerville to the Admiralty for his immediate attachment to the new department. And he could still hear the Admiral's parting words:

"I want results, and I want them soon."

So started the celebrated Wheezers and Dodgers department, which in the following four years were to work on a wide array of projects—several fundamental to the success of D-Day.

It would be four long years before this first tiny Allied step toward regaining the offensive would culminate in the great assault which would be flung against the Normandy beaches. Yet it would not be long before Allied commanders would be thinking of the actuality of returning Allied soldiers to the Continent. Actually, within less than a month of Dunkirk, in fact the very night after France signed a separate armistice with Germany on June 22, 1940, British troops stepped ashore again on French soil. True, this was only a reconnaissance raid near Boulogne by 120 Commandos, but it was a beginning nevertheless. The number was to have been 200, but enough boats of a suitable kind could not be found—despite the fact that a few weeks earlier one-third of a million men had been snatched from the smoke and death of Dunkirk. The raid provided little intelligence, and one group mistook their port of return in England—to be promptly arrested as deserters by the ever-vigilant British military police!

Yes, D-Day was still nearly four years off. But during July, Mr. Churchill set up a Combined Operations Command to conduct regular small raids on enemy coasts. Then in October he instructed the Joint Planning Staff to study the whole question of an offensive in Europe, even mentioning a bridgehead on the Cherbourg peninsula. But this was essentially a period of preliminary planning, for with the Luftwaffe still strong and active over England the possibility of a German invasion could not yet be completely ignored. The British could only look ahead to a time when they would have equal or superior land and air power, and try to keep the Atlantic open for supplies. For as German Admiral Raeder rightly said on December 27, 1940, "Britain's ability to maintain her supply lines is definitely the decisive factor for the outcome of the war."

Then Hitler invaded Russia in June, 1941, and the Communists in Britain almost immediately were echoing the pleas of Stalin, who had no hesitation in asking Churchill for a second front in France irrespective of the ability of the British to launch one. Only a year had passed since Dunkirk, but it would take two or three more before sufficient forces were built up in Britain to contemplate an attack on the Continent.

The day after the second anniversary of the outbreak of the war between Britain and Germany, Stalin told Churchill, "The Germans consider the danger in the West a bluff and are transferring all their forces to the East with impunity."

Churchill's reply was to point out that all his military advisers insisted that even if an attack were made in the West it could not succeed and would actually result in a withdrawal after a few days. And in a cable to Sir Stafford Cripps, the British ambassador in Moscow, Churchill revealed that far from being able to invade Europe, Britain still had to contend with the chance of an invasion by Germany in the spring of 1942.

Meanwhile, soon after the Stalin message of September 4, Churchill told the Joint Planning Staff "to complete as a matter of urgency their examination of the plan for operations on the Continent in the final phase, with particular reference to the requirements of all types of special craft and equipment both for the actual operations and for the training of the necessary forces."

Almost to the day, the Joint Planning Staff produced its first outline for an invasion of France in the summer of 1943, so when Churchill met Roosevelt in Washington on Christmas Eve for the Arcadia Conference of 1941, with the United States now committed to the war as a result of Japanese treachery at Pearl Harbor, they had this basis for discussion. There was also much else to talk over, and the conference lasted three weeks altogether. It was here that a common command to be called the Combined Chiefs of Staff was set up to pool all resources. And, secondly, the conference made a momentous decision to concentrate the efforts of the Allies against Germany before Japan. For the European situation looked as bad as it had been, with the Germans near Leningrad, Moscow and Sevastopol, and no one knowing if the Russians could withstand the Wehrmacht. Simultaneously, the Battle of the Atlantic reached its most serious stage, in one month during this winter eighty-eight ships being lost there and in the Arctic.

It was good to know that President Roosevelt saw the wisdom of the Germany-first strategy and also had the courage to endorse it at a time when his countrymen were more disposed to retaliate against the Japanese than turn to Europe. But even at the start there was considerable opposition to this "Europe First" strategy among the naval chiefs of the American High Command. It would continue to be a force to reckon with in all Allied planning, and would seriously affect the eventual invasion of France.

12

Nevertheless, by the spring, Roosevelt was becoming anxious for some sort of second front in Europe during 1942, and on March 9 cabled to Churchill that the losses involved "will be compensated by at least equal German losses and by compelling the Germans to divert large forces of all kinds from Russian fronts." So Churchill heard the cry for a second front from both of his main allies.

The Americans spent a considerable time deciding where to recommend this second front in Europe. They clearly could not get American troops to Russia; attacks through Scandinavia or Spain each presented problems; any decisive invasion via North Africa and Italy was too far from Germany to be effective; in fact the only possible place to start was from England. Apart from its obvious advantage of being directly opposite occupied Europe, England was also the nearest point for the transatlantic trip from the East Coast of the United States.

Against this axiomatic truth, however, many soldiers and statesmen held that the Atlantic Wall being built up by the Germans in France could not be broken with such an assault direct from the Channel shores of England. In fact, only a very few American officers thought it conceivable. Eisenhower was one of the small select group who believed in it, envisaging how air support coordinated with ground attack could create an invincible weapon for the ultimate liberation. Yet "ground" officers out of prejudice refused to realize the full possibilities of air power allied to their forces.

Throughout March the various viewpoints were exchanged, but by April 1 the American Operations Division, under Eisenhower, charged with preparing an offensive strategy, finally submitted an outline to the Chief of Staff, General George C. Marshall. The crux of their scheme was the establishment of overwhelming air power to be numbered in thousands of planes, so that the enemy air force and their land defenses could both be neutralized as completely as possible for the eventual invasion.

The Chief of Staff approved the scheme, conferred with Admiral King and General Arnold, and then sought the seal of the President. This Operations in Western Europe plan actually received Roosevelt's approval in one day, and he told Marshall to take the plan and Harry Hopkins to the British government.

Just one week later the two men arrived in London to advocate action in Europe at the earliest possible date. The British government agreed about Marshall's aim for a full-scale invasion in the spring of 1943, but his second suggestion of a landing in France during the present year "as a sacrifice to avert an imminent collapse of Russian resistance" met with direct disapproval. While sympathizing with the intention, Britain could not really contemplate an Allied landing in 1942, particularly when Marshall admitted that it would be late autumn before even the minimal level of troops, equipment and craft could be ready. October was not a good month to launch such an operation, nor the winter a suitable season to maintain it.

On April 14, Marshall was persuaded to abandon the idea of a bridgehead landing in 1942 unless the situation on the Russian front made such a desperate gamble necessary. At the same meeting, America and Britain made the historic agreement that, whenever the time came, the cross-Channel invasion was to be the main offensive operation in Europe. Neither knew that another twenty-six months would elapse before it could be begun.

Back in Washington, Marshall directed Eisenhower to visit London to bring back recommendations for organizing future American forces in Britain. Eisenhower found that the United States Commander in England had been given no chance to familiarize himself with the war in Europe as it would affect America. Suspended in London, the Commander was too far from the Pacific for it to mean much to him, and the United States had not yet transferred its attention to the European theater.

After a ten-day tour, Eisenhower returned to Washington, arriving on almost the same day as Molotov, who was belatedly accepting an invitation from President Roosevelt. The Russian at once told Roosevelt and Marshall that the Red Army might not be able to hold out against Hitler. If Britain and the United States could create a second front to draw off forty German divisions, however, chances might be better. Roosevelt listened to Molotov politely and then asked Marshall if he could tell Stalin that the

Allies were preparing a second front. Marshall agreed and the President authorized Molotov to tell Stalin that they expected a second front that year. In later talks, Roosevelt reminded Molotov that this must mean a reduction in Lend-Lease ships for Russia in the next twelve months. The Russian refused to accept this, and also managed to persuade the Americans to a communiqué which said:

"In the course of the conversations full understanding was reached with regard to the urgent task of creating a second front in Europe in 1942."

Marshall advised Roosevelt to omit "in 1942," but Molotov managed to keep it in the text. On his way home via London, Molotov received an assurance that Britain was preparing for a landing on the Continent in August or September, 1942, but could give no promise to do so.

While Molotov negotiated in Washington, Eisenhower was busy there too, drafting his "Directive for the Commanding General, European Theater of Operations" in which he envisaged unified command of all American forces in Europe. On June 8, he submitted it to Marshall, remarking that the general should study it in detail in view of its importance. Marshall replied:

"I certainly do want to read it. You may be the man who executes it. If that's the case, when can you leave?"

Eisenhower expressed amazement at these words, which apparently came to him as a complete surprise. Three days later he heard definitely that the appointment had been confirmed. His immediate reaction was to express dismay at the weight of responsibility involved, but he had little time to worry in the twelve hectic days that followed. In meetings with the Secretary of State, Eisenhower got the impression that the Secretary was anticipating that active operations would be started very soon, so he felt compelled to comment on the long build-up which would have to precede any attack.

Among the many things he had to do before leaving, Eisenhower called on Roosevelt and Prime Minister Churchill, a White House guest at the time; this was his first personal talk to either leader and despite the defeat at Tobruk which had just been announced, they both seemed cheerful as they concentrated on the coming struggle for liberation.

It was at this June meeting between the two that Churchill stressed strongly to the Americans the impossibility of an invasion of the Continent that year. The only major Anglo-American amphibious operation could be in French North Africa. And with the fall of Tobruk, Rommel headed toward El Alamein and Egypt, an advance which also sent Churchill hurrying back to London.

Then, on June 23, General Eisenhower flew off to Britain with General Mark Clark and some assistants and at once assumed command of the European Theater of Operations, U.S. Army, then comprising two countries—Britain and Iceland.

The commander could hardly have chosen a worse month to arrive, for shipping losses had been worse than in any other month so far. Merchant ships were being sunk at the devastating rate of one every four hours. And still the popular cry for a second front echoed everywhere although all the troops Eisenhower had in the United Kingdom consisted of two divisions and some small detachments of the U.S. Air Force, being trained in Northern Ireland. Little of the equipment necessary to contemplate any form of invasion existed, and some of the landing craft, far from being built, had still to be designed. Although this would have been bad propaganda for the public to hear, Eisenhower soon appreciated that no full-scale operation could be contemplated before mid-1943 and that unless almost all Anglo-American production were aimed at this single goal, it would be 1944 before the task of liberating Europe could be begun.

Independence Day, 1942, aptly marked the date of the very first American offensive operation by air against the enemy in Europe. Four German airdromes in Holland formed the target, and from a force of six Bostons—part of a bigger British group— two were shot down in a furore of flak. So four American crews remained. Obviously this was scarcely the time to talk of invasion. Eisenhower visited these crews on their return and later made his way thoughtfully back to London, where his headquarters was an apartment building near Grosvenor Square, already the center of American activity in London. The week of the Holland raid, after talks with British leaders, Eisenhower had to report to Washington that Britain would not consider any cross-Channel attack that year.

The U.S. Chiefs of Staff at once advised Roosevelt to concentrate on bringing about the defeat of Japan. Eisenhower's message reached General Marshall on July 10, and the U.S. Secretary of War wrote in his diary:

"The British War Cabinet ... are seeking now to reverse the decision which was so laboriously accomplished when Mr. Churchill was here a short time ago ... I found Marshall very stirred up and emphatic over it ... and he proposed a showdown which I cordially endorsed. As the British won't go through with what they agreed to, we will turn our backs on them and take up the war with Japan."

Marshall and Admiral King, another advocate of the Japan-first attitude, presented a plan to Roosevelt five days later for prosecuting the Pacific war. The President refused to accept it, however, and sent the two of them to London with Harry Hopkins to appeal again for Operation Sledgehammer, the name of the proposed bridgehead invasion of Europe. If Britain would not agree that this was feasible, then they were to settle for an offensive in French North Africa.

Long Anglo-American discussions began on July 18 to decide which of three possible offensives to undertake: aid the British forces in Africa via the Cape of Good Hope route; attack French North Africa to catch Rommel from the rear; or launch a limited bridgehead on the Channel coast of France. The British view—supported strongly by facts—was that German defenses put the Pas de Calais out of the question. Marshall argued for the Cherbourg Peninsula, and the fact that even an unsuccessful landing was preferable to inactivity. Eisenhower at that time also favored the cross-Channel bridgehead, although subsequently he came to appreciate that the British viewpoint was wiser. So native caution triumphed over the natural enthusiasm and eagerness of the Americans to attack in Europe there and then although enough landing craft existed to carry only one division!

After four days of bitter argument, Britain decided definitely against Sledgehammer. Then on July 24, the Allies agreed to proceed with planning Operation Torch, the invasion of North-West Africa. On the next day, Roosevelt cabled his approval of the plan which was to be put into operation not later than October 30. And then on the next day—with no time to lose—in his headquarters at Claridge's Hotel a few hundred yards down Brook Street from Grosvenor Square, Marshall appointed Eisenhower as commander in chief of Torch. This operation was not in fact launched until early December, but even then marked an amazing achievement.

And the direct-assault invasion? After he heard of the proposal for Torch, Stalin agitated less than before, although he still said that it ought to be possible to attempt a second front in France. At this precise time the Canadians carried out the reconnaissance attack against Dieppe, and exactly two-thirds of the 5,000 men involved became casualties: practical proof for Russia and America alike of what might have happened to a larger-scale invasion at any time in 1942. Yet the attack taught the Allies much more than they could have learned otherwise, and when D-Day came countless lives were saved through the sacrifice of the Canadians who died at Dieppe.

Two

"PLAN for the offensive . . . never think defensively," Churchill told British Vice-Admiral Lord Louis Mountbatten. And now as the war went on relentlessly day by day, Combined Operations, now under Mountbatten, was gaining valuable experience in offensive landings by raids on places as far apart as Vaagsö in Norway and St. Nazaire in France. Mountbatten reported direct to the Premier whenever necessary.

In May, 1942, three ideas important to the ultimate establishment of the Second Front were conceived. First, the Combined Commanders were appointed to overcome the problem of amphibious assault. Secondly, the British Wheezers and Dodgers first formulated the floating roadway, or "Swiss Roll," to link ships with shore by means of 1,000-foot sections of flexible metal roadway which was transported in monster rolls about a spindle, then unwound and laid by special barges with cranes over rafts which floated under each junction. And thirdly, Churchill revealed once more his astounding vision in science as in other things.

Long before the complete idea of the artificial Mulberry Harbors had been born, Churchill sent a memorandum to the Chief of Combined Operations on the kind of piers which would be needed at such ports. Not only did he predict the shape of these "mechanical monsters," as Gerald Pawle calls them, but also the principle on which they must work.

Churchill's memorandum is dated May 30, 1942, and appended to this a report on *Piers for use on beaches.*

Conditions of Beach

Average gradient is 1 in 200 and beaches are open to the southwest.

19

Conditions of Tide

Range of spring tides is 30 feet and the strength of the tide parallel to the beach is 4 knots at springs.

Scaffolding Piers

A pier to be of use for unloading ships of 20 foot draught would have to be 1 mile in length and 40 feet in height at the seaward end. The present type of scaffolding pier does not exceed 20 feet in height. It is doubtful whether a pier of these large dimensions could be made with scaffolding, but in any case the amount of material required would be prohibitive.

Pontoon Piers

A pontoon pier would have to be similar in length. All floating piers suffer from the disadvantage of having to be securely moored with heavy anchors. Even then they are most vulnerable and will not stand up to a gale of wind. The strength of the tide is so great that the moorings will have to be very large. If large pontoons were moored, 20 yards apart, at least 200 anchors would be required. The seaward end of a floating pier must be particularly well moored and the mooring chains form an obstacle to ships coming alongside. Owing to the poor ratio between the weight of a floating pontoon and the weight they can carry, and to their vulnerability to sea, wind and tide, they are not favoured in comparison with scaffolding piers on open beaches.

Churchill added to his memorandum to the Chief of Combined Operations:

They *must* float up and down with the tide. The anchor problem must be mastered. The ships must have a side-flap cut in them, and a drawbridge long enough to overreach the moorings of the pier. Let me have the best solution worked out. Don't argue the matter. The difficulties will argue for themselves.

Later it will be shown how the Whale on stilts fulfilled practically all Churchill's requirements.

Nothing seemed too small or too broad for Churchill's attention, and from the detailed study of piers for the invasion he turned in December, to the whole offensive outline.

In a telegram to Stalin, he declared:

"We must decide at the earliest moment the best way of attacking Germany in Europe with all possible force in 1943."

Stalin replied that he agreed but could not leave Russia for such a conference at that time. Churchill and Roosevelt therefore decided to proceed with a Combined Chiefs of Staff meeting, which was held in January, 1943. Even now the state of the war did not make it clear whether the Allies should attack Germany or Japan first. But Casablanca did determine by cold facts and figures that the long-mooted invasion could not now be commenced before the spring of 1944. The year or so intervening would be devoted to detailed planning and preparation for D-Day, coupled with redoubled efforts against Germany both in the underwater war with the U-boats and by an even heavier air assault on her industrial power.

Churchill stressed the value of the Mediterranean as a base "to strike at the underbelly of the Axis." An offensive against Italy would, he held, deflect Germany both from the Russian front and the French coast, and so soften the northern invasion route when it came to final fruition. Once again the Americans disagreed with British policy completely, thinking more of current Japanese successes than the ultimate Allied goal. But as usual Roosevelt saw more clearly than some of his service experts, in appreciating that the Mediterranean was a necessary prelude and part of the liberation, and agreement was reached as far as Eisenhower leading his American force in Operation Husky, the invasion of Sicily. But beyond that, the United States would not and did not commit itself, and as Chester Wilmot observes, the American High Command unfortunately assumed that Eisenhower would not require large numbers of landing craft after the conclusion of Husky. One last phrase emerged at Casablanca, the statement that the President and the Prime Minister both had as their objective "unconditional surrender" by Germany, Italy and Japan.

Toward this end, Lieutenant General F. E. Morgan was appointed Chief of Staff to the Supreme Allied Commander—happily shortened to COSSAC—at the Casablanca conference.

COSSAC went straight into action on all possible projects linked with the invasion. One of the vital needs exposed by Dieppe was for powerful, close support for the troops of so shattering a nature that the enemy defenses would be swamped between the time the naval bombardment ended and the moment when the first wave of troops touched the beaches. The COSSAC planners therefore decided that, as essential protection, the assault troops must be accompanied by their own floating artillery: hence was born the most ferocious and formidable weapon ever to bombard an enemy shore, the "Rocket Landing Craft."

Tests began on April 11, 1943, in the gray watery wastes off the Isle of Wight to see how strong a concentration of rocket fire could be achieved from a specially adapted tank-landing craft. On this first test the maximum achieved was 198 rockets fired in six groups of thirty-three each at intervals of half a second.

The results of this test indicated that members of operational crews in exposed places would be badly burned if the complete banks of rockets were fired at once. Moreover, the rockets still to be fired would be subjected to flame and hot gases which might well detonate their explosive. To see that the commanding officer of the rocket ship should be safe, the scientists recommended an enclosed kiosk, like a telephone booth, on the upper deck, and they also suggested that the ship's ack-ack gunners be issued asbestos clothing.

Despite these precautions, the problem of heat needed further examination, and so on April 21 they carried out more trials— this time by remote control, with the temperature gauges planted about the craft.

In eleven seconds, 759 rockets soared into the sky at an identical angle. Smoke swirled around the craft, flame cracked across its bridge, and a flood of melted red paint poured through cracks in the deck and smothered all the instruments placed "safely" below. Despite this mishap, other instruments near the rockets recorded 800 degrees, and when an electrical fault led to two salvos firing almost simultaneously the heat went up to 1,000 degrees!

One week later, on April 28, with more protective measures incorporated, the third trial took place off Portsmouth. This time a slight stern wind was blowing and the bridge kept cooler, but the deck and projectors became hotter than ever—so much so that on a warm day the risk of a general explosion in the craft would be high.

At the start of May, therefore, they tried out a solution to the heat in a dramatic manner—by flooding the whole deck with sea water during the firing period of the rockets. This unorthodox plan worked well and production plans started to convert thirty landing craft into rocket ships, each capable of carrying and firing a full salvo of over a thousand rocket shells: a withering weapon destined to be devastatingly successful in the ultimate invasion and even earlier in the Mediterranean landings later in 1943.

Three

ONLY a year left now and so much still to be done. Yet it was May of 1943 that marked the real beginning of this battle against time and a thousand obstacles: a fight for a second front in the summer of 1944. Now the signs of offensive began to be seen on all sides. On May 1, the British 6th Airborne Division, a new formation, came under the command of Major General Gale. By May, also, all Germans and Italians on the African continent had been killed or captured; Stalingrad had stopped the Germans on the Eastern Front; and the Allies accounted for forty U-boats in the everlasting minute-by-minute conflict on the seas.

By the end of May, another meeting of the Anglo-American High Command in Washington fixed the target date for D-Day as May 1, 1944. Operation Overlord at last assumed reality. There was an actual date to aim at—less than a year ahead. All was not yet agreed, however, for the Americans still did not favor carrying the North African fight into the "underbelly" by invading Italy. Their eyes remained on France and the Pacific, whichever way round the two were placed. In the end, all that the Americans would yield was that Eisenhower should "mount such operations in exploitation of the attack on Sicily as might be calculated to eliminate Italy from the war."

Churchill got Roosevelt to arrange to have General Marshall accompany the Prime Minister and General Sir Alan Brooke to Algiers to talk with Eisenhower about the extent of the forthcoming campaign. Churchill wanted "nothing less than the capture of Rome." Eisenhower reserved his judgment until he saw the strength of the opposition in Sicily, to be invaded on July 10.

Within a week of this date Eisenhower had made up his mind. Italy should be assaulted.

The entire conquest of Sicily took only thirty-eight days and apart from its obvious scheme in the over-all plan for victory in Europe it gave the Allies further vital experience with seaborne invasion. For the success of the operation, considerable credit was due the new amphibious load-carrier, the American DUKW; and equally to the LST, tank-landing ship. The latter was a new design based on British experience, built in the United States, and undergoing its first operational role in Sicily. All major amphibious assaults after this time had the LST as their foundation and their limitation.

From Malta and many African ports between Bizerta and Benghazi the landing craft came, but the weather was particularly bad, with a wind blowing and a heavy swell rolling into the Sicilian shores from the Mediterranean. Yet the convoys of small craft met it somehow and although delayed, damaged and scattered, they survived the night's crossing to find next morning that the wind had dropped leaving only a swell and surf on the western beaches of Sicily.

While the seaborne assault went well, Sicily marked a moment of tragedy for airborne forces. More than one-third of the gliders carrying the British 1st Air Landing Brigade were cast off too early by their American towing aircraft and many of the men they carried were plunged into the sea, trapped, and drowned. . . . Yet despite it all, Sicily meant much to Eisenhower, both in terms of contributing to changing his mind about an invasion of Italy, and also for the vital experience he gained before the great invasion of the next summer.

Meanwhile work went on throughout England, and even on the Continent, for D-Day. Some of the earliest activities were by small parties of men who paddled ashore in canoes at night to test the defensive strength of various beaches in Holland, Belgium and France. In addition to reconnaissance, they sought to survey the beaches, but as they landed literally under the enemy's nose, they could not employ normal surveying methods. Nor could they make the slightest sound.

26

So Combined Operations asked the Wheezers and Dodgers to devise a Beach Gradient Meter: a small truck which they could carry easily, push up and down the beach, and which would record on a paper down inside it a graph of the gradient of each particular beach. Combined Operations added a pathetic little footnote asking that the wheels should not squeak! The Wheezers and Dodgers created this cart, which accompanied the paddling parties to many alien shores, and once there they were able to record a complete contoured map of the beach they visited. By such strange means, valuable help was given toward the final decision on which would be the best areas for invasion.

It is obvious that the location of the assault was a prime problem, but once the Seine Bay became the agreed area, in January, 1943, the problem of the creation of a harbor where none naturally existed took over as the most vital and also the most difficult obstacle facing the Allies. On the flat open beaches of Normandy, even a breeze could churn the Channel into an awkward surf. And as Combined Operations Headquarters observed, this would make landing men an operation of great hazard, and delivering stores practically impossible. Without a harbor, the whole enormous enterprise would be jeopardized and might even be doomed. So paramount was the provision of a harbor that a report to the First Sea Lord called it "the crux of the whole operation."

At this stage two things were sure: there were no natural harbors on the beaches earmarked for landings, and no one knew exactly how to make artificial ones. Yet before D-Day they had to exist.

The poor planners of COSSAC were worried, with considerable cause. Not only had the Germans had four years to perfect their coastline defense, but as long also to plan the destruction of every port which the Allies could conceivably use. Then there was the Channel, unpredictable even in May or June. Thus they could not fairly face the prospect of an amphibious assault 100,000 men strong over only the open beaches of the Seine Bay. Five thousand ships would be involved, and bad weather would make it impossible to unload from landing craft and DUKWs. Everything

27

seemed against an artificial harbor, including a rise and fall of tide as much as 24 feet at springs. Thus any breakwater based in thirty feet of water at low tide would have to be fifty-four feet tall to reach the surface at high water. Yet somehow the Allies had to create two prefabricated harbors—each the size of Gibraltar—in little over a fortnight from the time they were towed across the Channel.

In April, Lieutenant-Commander Robert Lochner, R.N.V.R., was pondering this problem of artificial harbors when he suddenly realized that a wall in the sea need not be taken right down to the sea bed, but only as far down as the point where the waves lost their power. So the answer could be a *floating* wall.

From his original ideas, and after a hundred tests with models, three full-size floating breakwaters were being built in Portsmouth Dockyard during August, each 200 feet long and 12 feet wide.

Meanwhile, the wave formations of possible Mulberry Harbor sites were being examined, mooring experts determined the best way of securing long lines of floating objects close together offshore —and Churchill set out aboard the *Queen Mary* with his staff to meet the Americans again, this time in Canada. As he crossed toward Halifax, Nova Scotia, many things occupied his mind, but principally the preparations for Operation Overlord and the Italian campaign.

The pros and cons of the Pas de Calais or Normandy had finally been thrashed out, and it would be Normandy next year. Its defenses were less strong, the beaches reasonably favorable, and the immediate vicinity favored the movement of the large invasion forces—and yet was remote enough from the enemy's main forces. The coast between Havre and Cherbourg was well fortified with a mass of concrete forts and pillboxes, but the absence of a harbor here made it unlikely that the Germans would back up the defenses with large forces. Little did they dream that the Mulberry Harbors could materialize out of open sea and beach, but in April, 1943, Vice-Admiral John Hughes-Hallett originated the basic plan from all the current thought on the subject. What was the broad idea? Building in Britain equipment which could be carried across the

Channel in prefabricated form and transferred into harbors to sustain an invasion. On the beaches, great piers with their seaward ends afloat and sheltered where vessels could unload at all tides; protecting these, an arc of breakwaters enclosing an area of sheltered water for deep-draught ships. The breakwaters would be built of sunken concrete structures—code name Phoenix—and the revolutionary conception of scuttled blockships, known as Gooseberries. And as well as all these, the special scheme of floating breakwaters which was absorbing so much time and brainpower in London and Portsmouth. If the Mulberries could be brought into being, Churchill felt certain that the Allies would be able to unload at least 12,000 tons of equipment a day, enough to support an advancing army of one million, increasing to two million.

By the time the *Queen Mary* berthed at Halifax, he was well satisfied with the prospect of presenting the present picture to Roosevelt, which should convince the American authorities that Britain was doing all she could toward D-Day.

So began the Quadrant conference. Suddenly, about the middle of August, the Admiralty heard from Churchill that a team familiar with the floating breakwater was to fly to Quebec at once. Two War Office developers of the Whale Piers accompanied the group, which included Dr. William Penney and, of course, Lochner

After eighteen hours on hard straw mattresses in the bomb bay of a Liberator, they reached Quebec and drove to the Château Frontenac to find that a meeting on Artificial Harbors was due to start in a quarter of an hour! They had no alternative but to launch into technical conflict with the large American contingent there who were relying mainly on the use of sunken Liberty ships for the outer breakwater. When the unshaven British scientists pointed out that this was all based on a rise and fall in tide of only 18 feet, the theory collapsed. Up-to-date tidal information, Whale piers, and floating breakwaters—these three things cast a completely new light on the entire operation. The result was that the Mulberry project took practical shape. On his last day in America, Lochner gave a short talk on the breakwater to both Roosevelt and Churchill at the White House.

29

Four

EXPLODING enemy mine fields on beaches to be assaulted was an important invasion problem. On the same shores of Shoeburyness where Commander John Ouvry had conquered the German magnetic mine late in 1939, tests were made in 1941 to find out the effect of exploding charges in the air or ground level against land and beach mines. In the autumn of 1942 British Combined Operations hit on the idea that these charges might be fired from weapons mounted in a special landing craft. The result was the Hedgerow, composed of rows of spiky spigots set at different angles to be exploded at varying distances ahead of an assault landing craft on which they were mounted. One of these was ready in time to be tested in the Salerno assault in Italy on September 9. As a result of experience gained here, the elevations and projectiles were altered and the mountings strengthened and the Allies set to work in earnest to build Hedgerow flotillas for D-Day.

Secretly, steadily, momentum was gathering, and fleets numbering thousands of general landing craft began to take shape, well-designed, seaworthy craft instead of the ungainly ones used for the early British Commando raids which had proved unsuitably low-lying and liable to swamp in any substantial seaway. Actually these latter had really been obsolete when war broke out, because they had been the craft used at the Inter-Service Training and Development Centre, Fort Cumberland, Portsmouth, where the idea of a combined assault force had first blossomed. Most "modern" prewar developments like these had to be drastically reviewed in the light of conflict in the 1940's. When the Japanese used large landing-craft carriers bearing fleets of inshore landing craft against China, it began to be realized that landing vessels of every kind would be wanted to convey troops, guns, tanks and other armored vehicles.

Experimental craft went on to a hundred drawing boards and then as they were approved British and American shipyards and yacht-building centers built them almost in mass production. Where possible, parts were prefabricated at inland factories, and sent to assembly points around the coasts for incorporation. Cross-Channel packet boats of all sizes were requisitioned, converted, and fitted with specially strong davits to carry a number of inshore assault landing craft. Each of these L.S.I.s, landing ships infantry, could take several battalions of troops to within easy range of their objective and then lower the ten-ton assault landing craft into the water. Scrambling nets would also be lowered down the sides of the L.S.I.s so that the troops could man the L.C.A.s.

Literally dozens of different designs took shape between autumn, 1943, and the following spring. Another type of "flatiron" gunboat was the L.C.S., the support landing craft, designed to sail in ahead of the main landing parties to deal with immediate opposition. Early L.C.S. rather resembled midget submarines and were equally hard to see from a beach. A larger version was added to this armored boat.

L.C.P.s, personnel landing craft, were another development, though less impressive than the two monster vessels, the L.C.T., tank landing craft, displacing some 300 tons, and LST, tank-landing ship, ten times the size with 3,000 tons displacement. This latter vessel was being built to take troops as well as a load of 500 tons in tanks and heavy vehicles. L.C.T.s could also be converted into rocket, gun, and flak ships, in a similar way to the Hedgerow. And as the whole operation changed from broad aims to detailed development, the need appeared for still further craft: L.B.E.s, engineering landing barges, to make rapid running repairs along the beaches or in a more secluded spot, and L.C.K.s, kitchen landing craft, floating galleys for feeding the troops on the beachheads as soon as conditions allowed.

The jigsaw still seemed ragged, but at least the pieces were being cut, if not yet assembled in their proper places.

The British Commandos were not the only Royal Marines to be

preparing for D-Day, for in the late summer of 1943, when the Royal Navy found itself short of crews for the vast fleet of landing craft, the marines organized its light assault division into groups of men for these vessels. In less than six months, over 10,000 Royal Marines were trained to perfection and on D-Day about two-thirds of all the Allied assault craft landing the first waves of the army were manned by these marines.

The COSSAC plan at Quebec had proposed a three-division landing, with two airborne brigades to seize advance positions behind the enemy's coastal defenses. During the first fortnight, eighteen divisions were expected to be landed, after which main American army forces could then be shipped straight from the United States. General Morgan observed that the operation would triumph only if the Germans had not more than twelve reserve mobile field divisions in France, causing Molotov to inquire, when told of it:

"And what if there are thirteen?"

Operation Anvil was also agreed upon as a result of Quebec; a diversionary assault in southern France in the Toulon-Marseilles area.

The plan, the landing craft, and now the naval commander. In October, 1943, British Admiral Bertram Ramsay, back from the invasion of Sicily, became Allied Naval Commander in Chief, Expeditionary Force. From Dunkirk to Sicily, and now Normandy and Operation Neptune. One of Ramsay's headaches was destined to be obtaining enough ships—basic but far from automatic. Shipping for five divisions seemed possible: COSSAC wanted ten divisions. General Sir Alan Brooke told Morgan:

"It won't work but you must bloody well make it."

The same advice might have applied to Ramsay's task.

Ramsay's other main headache was Mulberry, but here the backroom boys rose to the occasion. Following the Quebec Conference, they had to build and test over two miles of the floating sea barrier. Yet this was only part of the problem of Mulberry. In addition fifteen thousand workmen had to be found to build the Phoenix concrete caissons forming the inner breakwater.

When Ramsay assumed command that autumn, he at once chose

33

Rear Admiral William Tennant to coordinate the many naval needs for Mulberry. And Tennant soon saw that there would not be enough room for the thousands of small supporting craft inside the sheltered waters during the early stages, and that additional breakwaters formed by blockships would definitely be needed. These blockships would be sailed across the Channel under their own steam and then sunk in line. So sixty old ships had to be found and manned in the next six or seven months to transform Gooseberry Harbors from fancy into reality.

By this time it had been determined that 96 full-scale Bombardon floating breakwaters, as they were called, were needed for the two Mulberry Harbors planned. This meant: 25,000 tons of steel, 1,000 tons of nuts and bolts, and 1,700 men for the six months remaining to D-Day.

The job began at docks in Tilbury and Southampton, and when the first two prototypes were built by the end of the year, they were towed to Newhaven, and moored there. But in a sudden winter gale off this exposed strip of Sussex shore both units broke their backs. Intensive detective work soon revealed the flaws, however, and by the end of January, 1944, fresh floating units, suitably strengthened, were towed to Weymouth Bay.

All this took time, and it was April 1 before the first full-scale trial started. With April came a strong sou'wester, an ideal test for the breakwater. Rough, rolling seas swirling in around Portland Bill toward Weymouth. But the Bombardons smoothed the waves so effectively that the next day the Admiralty received a message that the floating harbor had for ten hours withstood a stress twice as great as it was designed to meet, and repelled waves 8 feet high and 200 feet long.

Five

ON December 7, 1943, President Roosevelt passed through Tunis on his way back to the United States from Cairo, and Eisenhower went there to meet him. The President arrived in mid-afternoon and had hardly got into his car with the General before he announced:

"Well, Ike, you are going to command Overlord."

Eisenhower had already learned the lesson which was to stand him so well in his crusade in Europe—that war is waged in three elements but there is no such separate thing as land, air, or naval war. British Air Chief Marshal Tedder became his deputy commander with General Bernard Montgomery assigned as head of the British forces, and Air Chief Marshal Sir Trafford Leigh-Mallory as Air C in C. Admiral Ramsay, of course, had already been appointed. Roosevelt made Eisenhower's appointment known in a Christmas Eve broadcast, naming him Supreme Commander, Allied Expeditionary Forces. Soon after this, George C. Marshall summoned Eisenhower to Washington.

Until he could establish himself in London in the New Year, Eisenhower asked Montgomery to consider revising the initial ground plan for the beach assault, which seemed insufficiently strong since it was based on an initial attack force of only three divisions. He was glad to learn that Monty was working on a plan for a five-division effort. Meanwhile Eisenhower met Roosevelt once more. He found the President indisposed, but insisting that he had not felt better for years. Ike was never to see him again.

Eisenhower now flew back to London, arriving on the evening of January 14, and set about finding a suitable site for his H.Q.—Supreme Headquarters, Allied Expeditionary Force, shortened to

35

SHAEF. Soon he found the spot from which to command the mightiest fighting force ever to be assembled for one assault. Ironically it was within sight of Hampton Court Palace, with its timeless Tudor associations.

Eisenhower found to his relief that Montgomery had the new plan ready in principle, a plan contemplating the use of two or three airborne divisions followed by the main sea assault by five divisions, followed by two more immediately. The coastal frontage of the assault was thus doubled to 50 miles wide, requiring large increases in forces. Actually this would be easier decided than accomplished, for the Admiralty could scarcely meet the original COSSAC needs of 3,323 landing craft, 467 warships, and 150 minesweepers. With only three clear months before the target date of May 1, it was obvious that at least an extra month would be required to obtain more new landing craft straight from production, and also to allow time to divert craft from the Mediterranean to Overlord. Incidentally, the United States Navy allocated an impressive 2,493 craft to Overlord but this figure palls when it is realized that by now it possessed over 30,000 such craft.

Eisenhower endorsed the revised assault plan within a week of his arrival in England, and two days later notified the Combined Chiefs of Staff of the month's postponement. None of this was in any way his fault; rather, it could be blamed on the COSSAC organization, in particular on the American members who seemed always to be fighting for the Pacific. Even throughout February and March, the struggle for landing craft continued, and Ramsay had to plan half in the dark during these vital months.

Luckily other equipment was not quite so hard to obtain. Montgomery developed a Joint Fire Plan to saturate the beaches in a climactic crescendo just before the first troops waded in. To achieve this drenching fire, the landing craft had to have their own floating artillery of guns, mortars and rockets which had been developed as we have already seen.

The fire of this floating artillery also had to be supplemented by powerful amphibious armor. Dieppe had taught that tank support must be given from the first moment of D-Day, and General Brooke had formed an experimental armored division in March,

1943, to develop tank warfare as applied to the second front, and told its commander, Major General Sir Percy Hobart, to see that they had armor for the job. Hobart proceeded to prepare an imaginative range of vehicles. Bulldozer tanks to tackle beach obstacles; flail tanks to hammer a way through mines; tanks to attack concrete fortifications; weird turretless tanks for other tanks to use as ramps to scale sea walls; tanks carrying bridges and others throwing flames against pillboxes.

Most valuable and vital was the amphibious DD (Duplex Drive) tank able to invade on its own. The British Admiralty refused to believe that this DD design would ever actually swim in an exposed sea, or that it could be launched from landing craft. Despite demonstrations to the contrary by its Hungarian inventor, it was still spurned since it did not have a rudder!

Hobart took over five of these DD tanks, but these were the obsolete British Valentine type. The obvious choice for conversion to amphibious operation Brooke saw to be American Shermans, so he ordered the conversion of 900 in July, 1943. By January, 1944, Hobart saw that this number would never be available at the current conversion rate, despite Montgomery's enthusiasm for them. Then the Americans began to move. On January 27, Eisenhower saw the DD demonstrated. On January 28, an engineer was on his way to the United States with drawings of it. By February 4, American factories had actually begun work on the job. And by early April, 300 Shermans had been converted.

While Eisenhower was coming to grips with the race against time to invade Europe, Rommel was moved, in January, by Hitler to command two of the armies in the West. Von Runstedt remained the German commander in chief but soon Rommel became the real power behind the Atlantic Wall. It was he who would implement the German policy of which both Hitler and himself approved, that the Allied invaders must be repulsed as near the actual coast as possible. Apart from maneuvering troops accordingly, Rommel at once began to implement a scheme to impede any forces trying to land along the Channel coast, although he did not know precisely where the assault would occur.

By March, a whole assortment of wire entanglements, jagged

spikes, concrete teeth, and beach mines began to be identified by
Commando reconnaissance raids along the coast; posts and wires
were planted inland to deter airborne assault; artillery sites were
roofed in against attack, and a rash of new pillboxes appeared.
Rommel ordered the flooding of low-lying areas in the coastal belt,
an action especially successful in the marshy region around the
Carentan estuary, while existing sea walls were strengthened and
extended to try and stop tanks from landing.

Most serious of all, however, were the underwater obstacles
located at varying distances below the high-tide mark. With explosive charges attached to them, these were intended to impale
or cripple landing craft before they could reach the shore. After an
inspection by Rommel in March, construction on such defenses was
accelerated, the coastal batteries were increased, and new obstacles
were observed farther and farther out to sea. The anti-air-landing
obstacles grew more frequent on our reconnaissance photographs,
some being fitted with booby traps.

To man all these extra fortifications, Rommel had to sacrifice the
idea of a depth in defense, but this agreed with his policy in any
case. It gave rise to a storm among the German High Command,
however, and led eventually to a fatal compromise. Rommel wanted
to halt a hostile force by concentrating a violent volume of fire on
the beaches, and hammering home a counterattack by all available
reserves near the coast.

Von Runstedt preferred the crust-cushion-hammer principle:
a crust of infantry manning the coastline, a cushion of infantry
divisions in reserve in the rear, and a hammer of armored forces in
strategic reserve still farther inland. As it happened, the central
Panzer divisions were forced to engage the Allies too soon, and so
were unable to strike a coordinated blow at the right time and place.

As the underwater obstacles multiplied, it became clear once
and for all that the invasion could not possibly be mounted on the
beaches at night, and that even by day the risks were likely to be
great.

If high tide were chosen as the moment for the first assault, many
landing craft would be ripped or blown to bits by the mines and
traps. At low tide, on the other hand, the men would be exposed to

fearful fire across hundreds of yards of open beach. So half-tide was the only answer. To help cover the infantry, Montgomery decided to use armor early in the assault: DD tanks, then specialized armor, then the infantry. Flails would clear the way for the DDs and others. A complication arose here, though, for some of the beaches had patches of sticky clay well below high-water mark; one of Monty's advisers happened to remember this from a prewar holiday in the Seine Bay! Aerial photos picked out these patches, and Commandos slipped silently ashore one spring night and brought back samples. These were urgently analyzed and a comparable beach found in England where tests soon showed that tanks quickly became bogged. Hobart as usual came to the rescue and an antidote appeared: an attachment to a tank permitting it to lay a matting road across the clay for the rest to follow. Wherever clay was suspected, it was arranged that the leading tank should be a "bobbin," as the device was called.

In February and March, two midget British submarines, X.20 and X.23, took their place at the submarine base of Fort Blockhouse, Gosport, ready to help survey some of the beaches. It was X.20 which was the one lucky enough to undertake Operation Postage. The little vessel sailed submerged right into the Arromanches area of the invasion coast, and took depth soundings all along the sector, measured the beach gradients, and mapped as many underwater obstacles as they were able to in the time allotted, a period of several days.

After this, the two X craft prepared for their equally secret but more rewarding role of sailing ahead of the invasion to act as navigational marks for the whole armada.

Similar surveys to those by X.20 had also been carried out a little earlier by small personnel landing craft towed toward the French coast by motor launches.

Meanwhile work on another invasion project was proceeding well: Pluto. This was not Walt Disney's famous canine cartoon character, but the name in initials of the equally famous operation for supplying gasoline to the thousands of Allied vehicles once they were on French soil: Pipe Line Under The Ocean. Unlike some other invasion projects, this had been developed in good time, and by 1942, a thousand miles of pipes were already in position to carry fuel from Stanlow, on the Mersey, and Bristol to London and other southern ports.

From here the problem was how to extend this actually under the ocean. The back-room boys again came forward and, working under strict secrecy, developed a 3-inch-diameter pipeline which, after it passed all its tests, was subjected to sea trials to see how it would unwind.

The tests were successful and now production of Pluto began: four lines extending 70 miles each from the Isle of Wight to Cherbourg, which was due to be captured soon after D-Day. Later there would be seventeen lines more from Dungeness to Calais.

Men of the Royal Engineers and R.A.S.C. were trained to work pumping stations set up at the English terminal points, one of these pumping heads being provocatively placed in the cliffs immediately opposite Boulogne. Ships were found with holds big enough to house the massive pipeline, and landing barges earmarked to link up the main line, when it was laid, to the battle beaches. Over a thousand naval personnel were assigned to accomplish this unique job.

All over Britain signs of D-Day abounded. Allied troops trained literally from John o' Groats to Land's End, and tanks roared through quiet English villages, disturbing the dust of soft spring days. Civilian travel to and from Eire was stopped, to cut down the risk of espionage, and in April the whole coast from the Wash to Cornwall came under strict supervision. No visitors were permitted without reason and no residents could travel more than a certain distance from their own homes.

Since it would be impossible to camouflage the intentions of an armada—even though its ships might be camouflaged—there existed a vital need to mislead the enemy about the goal on D-Day, or at least to conceal it as long as possible. To help do this, dummy landing craft built specially for the purpose were berthed very visibly in Dover and other Cinque Ports, as well as Nore Commands. With these elaborate "blinds" went troop concentrations in Kent and Sussex to suggest preparations for a landing in the Pas de Calais area. The skyscraper effect of the tall Phoenix and Whale units at Selsey and Dungeness confirmed the enemy's idea that the Straits of Dover must be our intended location. And all this while the Allies made sure that they spread the ships and landing craft equally among ports of the British Isles, so that no abnormal concentrations could be observed by German aircraft along the coast opposite Normandy. All divisions not scheduled for early landing in France were trained and billeted in Kent, and German aircraft over this area duly reported both the dummy craft and the troops. Proof of this came from Intelligence, who reported enemy reinforcements of ten to fifteen divisions between Havre and Calais, while Brittany and the Mediterranean also received some.

Churchill, meanwhile, had recovered from flu and convalescence at Marrakesh, and was back in his old form. He expedited Montgomery's request to have vehicles waterproofed by a special process which would permit them to be driven through a few feet of water without harm on the Normandy shores.

He also kept in touch with Mulberry, especially watching progress of the twenty-three Whale floating pier units, which he had specified "must float up and down with the tide." The main Mulberry components were now an inner Phoenix breakwater of huge concrete caisson units which were to be towed across the Channel and sunk by opening release valves; and a series of the Whale floating piers. These ran out to Spud pierheads, also floating and mounted on great stiltlike legs which were designed to adjust to the height of the tide.

The Premier also encouraged the Mulberry project personally at a conference in late January at which it was decided definitely to augment the proposed two harbors with five Gooseberries—one in each divisional assault area—of sunken blockships which could be laid in place more quickly than the fortnight estimated for the complete Mulberries. At Churchill's suggestion, the United States agreed to supply nearly half of these ships.

At a service conference exactly two years earlier, Admiral Mountbatten had said:

"If ports are not available, we may have to construct them in pieces and tow them in."

He heard the idea jeered in derision, but fortunately for the

Allies, he was one of the select company whose vital vision helped win the war.

So it went on.

As soon as Intelligence reported the latest tactical obstacles the Germans were preparing for us, the Allies quickly copied them at a secret situation in East Anglia so that troops could be familiarized with them. Here they built pillboxes, stone walls and barbed wire; dug ditches such as tanks would face; laid mine fields; and erected steel obstructions. These were all replicas of enemy equipment. Not only did the Allied engineers study it, where possible they designed countermeasures which could destroy it. These were tried out in the field, where new battle techniques also first saw light.

The Bangalore torpedo, for instance, had frequently been fired across a mine field to detonate all mines in its route and so clear a path for advancing troops. Now a new way was being evolved, more in tune with the times of armored warfare. A Sherman tank was covered with a series of pipes, each with a Bangalore torpedo. These pipes pointed straight ahead, and as the tank advanced, it fired these unusual "guns" in sequence. The torpedoes were shot out and exploded ten yards in front of the vehicle, clearing a continuous track through the mines.

Sea and harbor, too, could be equally lethal, and already the Germans were claiming that in the first quarter of 1944 they had laid 165 million mines in the Bay of Caen alone. Whether or not this exaggerated the figure, it was obviously formidable, and plans to clear harbors had to be made so that when the Allies captured a port it would be workable. More specifically still, Cherbourg must be a key to ultimate Allied success after D-Day, but Cherbourg harbor was bound to be heavily sown with both booby traps and delayed-action mines which could not be swept normally and would have to be handled individually by frogmen.

But before this could even be attempted, some sort of special suit had to be devised to protect them as far as possible from the danger of death by underwater blast.

In only six weeks, these protective suits must be tested, made and distributed. To test them, naval personnel underwent a series of danger-fraught tests at Horsea Island, near Portsmouth. They were lowered into a deep salt-water lake, where they were subjected to explosions at varying depths and distances from their bodies to discover the effects. Often they were taken from the lake semiconscious, and suffering agonizing pains which lasted long afterwards. But thanks to their heroism, a protective suit was rushed into production and played its role at Cherbourg and elsewhere, when port parties had to clear hundreds of mines from enemy harbors. Many frogmen's lives were definitely saved by the suit so heroically tested at Horsea.

Another underwater development about this time was connected with the army's secret amphibious tank. No one had yet devised a means of escape for the crews of these monster vehicles should they sink at sea. In only three days, a lightweight escape apparatus was created and tested actually underwater by sinking one of the amphibians. This, too, served in saving lives on D-Day.

Six

PLANS were progressing on land and sea; the tempo was tenser, more electric. But D-Day could come to nothing without the Allied Air Forces. First of all, the ceaseless strategic bombing against German centers of industry and aircraft production inflicted such blows on the strength of the Nazi air force that for each of the five months from November, 1943, to March, 1944, less than half the planned production of single-engine fighters was actually achieved. At the same time, heavy attacks on airfields and losses suffered in combat cut the enemy's power still more. Thus the Allies gradually won control of the air over France in preparation for the invasion. This was not achieved without heartbreaking sacrifice by both the British and American air forces. On the night of March 30-31, 1944, ninety-four aircraft of British Bomber Command failed to return from an attack on Nuremburg.

By this time, however, the new American long-range fighters had mastered the enemy's during the day, and Allied bombers made powerful precision attacks, protected by American Thunderbolts, Lightnings, and later Mustangs.

Throughout the preliminary period before the final fling for D-Day, air attacks also had to be maintained on "Noball" targets, the code name for the German flying bomb and rocket-launching sites.

Important as all these objectives obviously were, the main aim was to stop enemy supplies from reaching the invasion area once the fight was on. To do this, the railway-bombing plan started in April. For if the enemy's railway system could be hit hard enough, they would not be able to supply or reinforce their troops. Thus the railway centers of northern France and the Low Countries were hit by 66,000 tons of bombs in three months, with the avowed aim of creating a "railway desert" around the Germans in Normandy. Secondary targets were the main marshaling yards while another part of the plan covered the destruction of road and rail bridges, including severing the Seine bridges below Paris and the bridges over the Loire below Orléans.

Eighty targets in all were attacked in this plan, fifty-one being heavily damaged, twenty-five damaged, four little affected.

The first full onslaught on a rail center took place on March 6-7, when the R.A.F. bombed Trappes. No less than 190 direct hits exploded on the actual tracks and the entire electrified line between Paris and Chartres was put out of service so completely that it still needed repairs two months later. Throughout March and into April, the story was the same: at Paris/Noisy le Sec, the whole railway complex was completely wiped out. A suppertime attack on Charleroi/St. Martin ploughed up the massive marshaling yards, which were still out of service on D-Day. Gradually a creeping paralysis extended over the whole northern network, west of Paris-Amiens-Boulogne and south Belgium.

Eastern routes to Paris received similar devastating attention in May, but the raids were restricted on several occasions because of the danger to French civilians. The vital junction of Le Bourget was not attacked at all, in fact, since heavy loss of life among the Allies would have been inevitable. Thus it was not yet total war.

Stupendous-scale fighter sweeps intercepted locomotives all over northern France. On May 21, over five hundred British-manned Thunderbolts with 233 Spitfires claimed 67 locomotives destroyed and 91 damaged. The Americans claimed 91 locomotives destroyed on the very same day.

Lines, locomotives, and also rail and road bridges leading into the assault area were preferred targets. This bombing of bridges had a twofold object: to check troops and supplies entering the battle, and also to prevent their making a rapid retreat should it become necessary to them. Leigh-Mallory had to take care not to betray any special interest in the routes to Normandy, however, so the bridges over the Seine became the first targets, together with others which did not commit the Allies to any specific assault area.

So the steady air attacks went on and forty-nine coastal batteries capable of firing on shipping approaching the assault area were bombed and blasted.

German radar by now spanned the entire coast from Norway to the Spanish border, by a chain of stations. These radar targets had heavy defenses, so low-level attacks were carried out by the R.A.F. 2nd Tactical Air Force. Many senior pilots died in these missions, but in so doing they saved the lives of many invading Allies the following week. Navigational and wireless telegraph stations also were subject to the same sort of accurate, shattering attack. Wires fell across the stations in a mesh of misty smoke and fire. Masts leaned over crazily and crashed down in a maze of metal.

Yet another major series of operations aimed at airfields in a radius of 150 miles of Caen, and the final three weeks or so between May 11 and D-Day every German airfield within that range was systematically bombed, yet without revealing that the Seine Bay would be the ultimate area to be invaded.

Constructive—as opposed to destructive—operations had their place in this amazing Allied air scheme. In fact, photographic reconnaissance units were some of the earliest people to be on active preparation for the invasion. For more than a year, complex information had been gathered which wanted careful collation to serve its purpose in the over-all plan. Damage assessment sorties after all major bombing raids was an obvious example of reconnaissance of such kind.

Apart from this, however, a patient, painstaking camera coverage was made of the entire occupied coast line from Holland down to the Spanish frontier to map details of defenses. Verticals and oblique angles were photographed of beach gradients, obstacles, coast defenses and shore batteries. Complete coverage from Granville to Flushing helped to hide our specially selected beaches.

Flying three to four miles out from the coast, aircraft took oblique pictures at wave-top height—often hazardously—to give assault coxwains a "landing-craft view" of their area. Then the planes came inshore to 1,500 yards from the coast, and at zero feet—waves all but washing their wingtips—they photographed again at oblique angles to provide platoon assault commanders with recognition landing points. Next, climbing steeply to 2,000 feet altitude they took more pictures from the same distance offshore to record views of the immediate hinterland in relation to the beaches.

Day in and out, the unspectacular work went on, right through the winter of 1943-1944 and until the spring. Inland strips were recorded behind the assault areas, bridges over rivers given special pictorial attention, and likely advance airfield sites photographed for future reference. More still: all dropping areas for our airborne divisions had to be accurately mapped from photos, and as Rommel stepped up his "defense offensive" throughout March, April and May, the booby traps, spikes, and so on, came under the all-seeing eye of the reconnaissance camera. Flooding had to be checked for change regularly; enemy supply dumps confirmed; and a mass of other detail done. They even photographed Allied landing craft and equipment at anchor in our ports to test the most effective camouflage. In the fortnight before D-Day, *one* R.A.F. Mobile Field Photographic Section alone made for Army requirements 120,000 prints!

While all these diverse air duties were being carried out, the actual Operation Overlord received an alarming threat. Reconnaissance reported in the autumn of 1943 that flying-bomb and rocket-launching sites could be detected under construction in the Pas de Calais and Cherbourg areas. Part of the Allied valuable air power had to be diverted to deal with them, and on December 5, 1943, sixty-three flying-bomb sites and five rocket sites received their baptism of bombing. The Pas de Calais sites were aligned on London and those around Cherbourg on Bristol. From then on, a steady stream of aircraft attacked a total of 97 flying-bomb sites, neutralizing 86. Two out of seven rocket sites were smashed. Although, as already well known, these secret weapons enjoyed some major successes, it is estimated that without the air assault on their sites, the fearful flow of 6,000 flying bombs per day might have been aimed at England. Under such a staggering attack, the Allies could hardly have begun an invasion.

The final figures for the two-months' softening-up operations of April, May, and to June 5, were 200,000 sorties by the combined

Allied air forces. So it was a question of offense and defense. As the spring sped on, more and more of the D-Day armada were gathering, inevitably very vulnerable, around the coast. All this time, protection against attack by air had to come partly from the Allied fighter force. For over 6,000 craft were to be employed during that first week after D-Day. Not only were the craft good targets, but equipment and troops, too, had to be assembled. Leigh-Mallory knew that Germany had 450 heavy bombers still on hand to hammer at the preparations for invasion, but for some reason a raid on this scale never materialized. Three phases of enemy air attack by night during April and May revealed that they knew of the general preparation for invasion, for all were directed at the South Coast.

On April 25-26, 40 German aircraft attacked Portsmouth and Havant; on the next night, 80 aircraft repeated the Portsmouth target and operated within a triangle of the Needles, Basingstoke and Worthing. Two nights later came Plymouth's turn. The second phase, in mid-May, made by 100 and 80 aircraft on successive nights, concentrated on Southampton and Weymouth. And the third phase at the end of May took the targets southwestward to Dartmouth and Start Point.

Apart from these efforts, the enemy's reconnaissance sorties were restricted to only some 125 in the six weeks before D-Day. So strong had the Allied air forces grown that these fleeting Luftwaffe flights rarely got farther than mid-Channel—probably deterred by permanent R.A.F. patrols flying as far out as forty to fifty miles south of the Isle of Wight.

This was just as well, too, for a considerable part of the initial invasion force was gathering in the Solent. This armada of unprecedented size swung at anchor, the vessels scarcely able to clear each other as they moved with the tide. Here was an amazing chance for the Germans to recoup their fading fortunes, but as so often before they muffed it with a compromise. If they could have showered only a comparatively small number of mines among these vessels, untold damage would have been caused. Minesweeping waters so tightly packed as these would have been almost impossible, so the ships could not have weighed anchor safely, or even swung to the Solent tide.

The Germans did try to mine the Solent area twice, on April 28 and May 15, but the raids caused no casualties nor inconvenience. The first time, white flare markers were dropped in the Needles channel well clear of any anchorage, while a strong tide was running. Mine-laying aircraft came over afterward and released their missiles on the flares, which by then had drifted into shallow water. Most of them thus exploded quite harmlessly since they were set to fire in these conditions so that they should not be taken intact. But to make matters easy, two of them did actually drift down without exploding at all and landed on British soil at Milford-on-Sea. These gifts were promptly photographed and stripped by officers of H.M.S. *Vernon,* the British Navy's Portsmouth base famous for rendering enemy mines safe.

The May mine-laying raid was aimed at the other end of the Isle of Wight, on the eastern Solent, but fighter aircraft aided by a ship's smoke screen completely frustrated the attempt. The only observed mines fell on land! So the armada grew daily, packed so tightly that it spread southward into St. Helen's Roads, near the area of this second mine-laying effort.

Yet another lost Nazi opportunity also concerned mines. By early 1944 the Germans had become very aware of the imminence of invasion, but of course could not guess where it would strike. So, as a protective measure, a large defensive field of moored mines was laid parallel to the coasts of Holland, Belgium and all northern France. But the Germans reckoned for certain that the Allies would invade during the first five months of the year. Thus, since they could not leave so widespread a mine field indefinitely as it would interfere with their own vessels around those coasts, every one of these mines was fitted with a flooder set for the end of May. The weeks went by—and still no invasion. Then at various times through the day of May 31, each of these thousands of mines in the great field flooded according to schedule, sank harmlessly to the bottom. It was a major mistake, for while they would not have saved the Germans, they must have meant more losses for the Allies.

Allied Bomber Command had its own silent mine-laying duties, too. As if to show the Germans how to carry out offensive operations, the R.A.F. laid over 3,000 ground mines in areas along the Dutch, Belgian and French Coasts, east of Texel, and in Baltic and German waters. The aim was to bottle up as many naval outlets as possible, so that the Germans had as few ships as possible free to intercept the invasion fleet. The operations were highly successful. Some of the credit belongs to the brilliant scientists attached to H.M.S. *Vernon* who devised the complex acoustic and magnetic mines, and combinations of both, that all but defied sweeping. Throughout that spring, mines were assembled with circuits which were constantly changed to mislead the enemy's sweeping plans.

Meanwhile, one other enemy air attack was aimed at the battleship *George V* in Plymouth. The Germans used a new type of radio bomb, which was controlled by the observer in the aircraft making the attack. Luckily, this proved just as unsuccessful as the mine-laying raids in the Solent.

Seven

On New Year's Day, 1944, Montgomery handed over his command of the British Eighth Army and took off from the Sangro River airstrip in Italy.

First he was flown to Marrakech where Churchill—recuperating from pneumonia—confronted him with the COSSAC plan. Montgomery's reaction was that the assaulting forces would not be powerful enough. Arriving next day in England he at once began studying the plan in detail, thus confirming his opinion both as to the lack of strength and the too confined nature of the assault.

Basically the invasion plan was to assault the Normandy coast north of the Carentan estuary and also between the estuary and the River Orne. This would yield a base for further operations to include taking airfield sites and the port of Cherbourg.

Once ashore and firmly footed in France, Montgomery's idea was to threaten to break out on the eastern flank, in the Caen sector. This would draw the main enemy reserves into that area, where the British and Canadian armies would keep them fully occupied. Once these reserves had been committed to the East, he would break out on the West, with the American armies under General Bradley pivoting on Caen. This break-out attack would be delivered dramatically southward down to the Loire and would then swing east in a wide sweep up to the Seine about Paris. This would cut off all enemy forces south of the Seine, leaving them without bridges back over the river since these had been destroyed by air action. The two keys to the entire situation were the rapid advances necessary in the West, and the immense importance of Caen in the East.

Before Montgomery went into detail he naturally considered the exact enemy situation in north France and how it would influence his strategy. The German army groups finally opposing him on D-Day numbered some 60 divisions, but these varied in quality from SS and Panzer formations down to low-quality static coast defense forces. Montgomery received reports of all the elaborate defense measures, including the formidable Element C: the underwater obstacles with Teller mines on the forward face. Monty also had a shrewd idea of the respective ideas of Rommel and Von Runstedt, whose conflicting conceptions resulted in the compromise already mentioned. Another handicap to the Germans proved to be the existence of a third army group in France called Panzer Group West. This administered the Panzer formations, which were operationally commanded by the other army groups: a system which not unnaturally led to some confusion in the over-all operation of enemy armor when the invasion was launched.

In the assault sector itself, Montgomery anticipated the enemy garrison to be three coast-defense divisions supported by four reserve divisions. He constantly reviewed both the build-up of possible enemy forces in the area and also their strategy. By D+6, the enemy should be able to concentrate up to twenty divisions in the Normandy area; D+20, Montgomery might expect twenty-five to thirty; and by D+60 up to fifty divisions.

Intelligence kept him posted with regular appreciations of German strength and in April and May they reported encouraging signs. Whereas in January, 1944, they had estimated that by D+60, the enemy would be able to move as many as fifteen divisions into the West from elsewhere in Europe, the level in April dropped to six, as a result of the Soviet successes and the turn of events in Italy. The picture brightened even more in May, as the Germans stood on the threshold of a three-sided siege: Russia, Italy, and soon France.

Meanwhile, Montgomery pored over maps of France, especially the Varreville sector. Among his hundreds of problems were the inundations behind the beaches of Varreville, which made the vital exits from beach to hinterland awkward. Here, for instance, he had to be sure the Allies would capture the causeways across flooded areas lest they be pinned down to the beach strip by small enemy forces.

The land behind the beaches generally favored defense, and was not suited to shifting large armored forces. But he had to try and overcome this. Apart from the open rolling plain southeast of Caen, the whole region was covered to a depth of thirty to forty miles inland by Bocage, that peculiar pastureland split up by high hedges, banks and ditches into small fields and meadows. It was ideal for infantry and sniping, but bad for tanks.

As Montgomery prepared his plan, the assault on Europe had really already been begun—by the devastating air attacks which were slowly strangling Germany's economy. Then came the road and rail bombardments, which were to be rewarded on D-Day by the remarkable report that every railway bridge over the Seine between Paris and the sea was impassable to the enemy. And all the time, the victory at sea in the Battle of the Atlantic, allowing the vast volume of American and Canadian men and materials over to take part.

What was this amazing assault to be? The invasion of a continent by 130,000 men and 20,000 vehicles was an event unheard of in the history of war. Their aim: to burst the barrier of the Atlantic Wall and to free Europe.

Simultaneous landings would be made by eight brigades—three British, two Canadian, three American, along with U.S. Rangers and British Commandos. Airborne troops were thrown in on both flanks: the American airborne divisions at the base of the Cotentin peninsula to help the battle of the beaches and then isolate Cherbourg; and a British airborne division to seize the crossings over the Caen canal on the extreme left.

The 1st U.S. Army was to assault astride the Carentan estuary, capture Cherbourg as quickly as possible, then drive south to Saint-Lô.

The 2nd British Army assault would develop the bridgehead south of the line Saint-Lô–Caen and southeast of Caen, to take airfield sites and protect the eastern flank of the American army aiming at Cherbourg. The United States attack would be on Utah and Omaha beaches, the British on Gold, Juno and Sword beaches.

During the night before D-Day, as the armada made its silent passage, intense air action against enemy defenses would begin, while airborne forces would be dropped on two flanks in advance of the mass assault on the next morning. At H-Hour, the leading waves of liberation forces would land under the stupendous support of naval bombardment, air action, and the guns, rockets and mortars of close-support craft. So eight brigades, combat forces, special assault engineers, amphibious tanks, and much more would beach on the first three tides.

Airlift priority went to American airborne troops whose vital job it would be to secure the beach exits from the Utah sector. Main bodies of them were to land near Ste. Mère Église on the night of D−1 Day, some to help the seaborne assault on Utah, others to intercept any movement of enemy reserves into the Cotentin peninsula.

The last lift was for British forces due to land before H-Hour east of Caen, east of which they were to dominate with the aid of the Commandos. American Rangers were to land in the assault on the west of Omaha beach to attack defenses on the east side of the Carentan estuary.

One British Commando brigade Montgomery earmarked to link the assaults on the Juno and Sword sectors. Another would land behind the assault on the Sword sector, and while part dealt with the village of Ouistreham, the rest would cross the Orne and attack enemy coast defenses of the river up to Cabourg.

The Allies had studied assault technique now for a long while and had rushed all the special equipment they found they needed into quantity production. They had the weapons, but what was the best way to use them?

Montgomery's answer was the Joint Fire Plan in which the resources of all three services were mobilized to see that the army got ashore. That was the first essential of D-Day. To do this, the plan proposed first to destroy or neutralize the enemy coast artillery batteries which might attack the approaching naval convoys or fire on the anchorages, and then wipe out all strong points and other localities sited for the immediate defense of the chosen assault beaches.

56

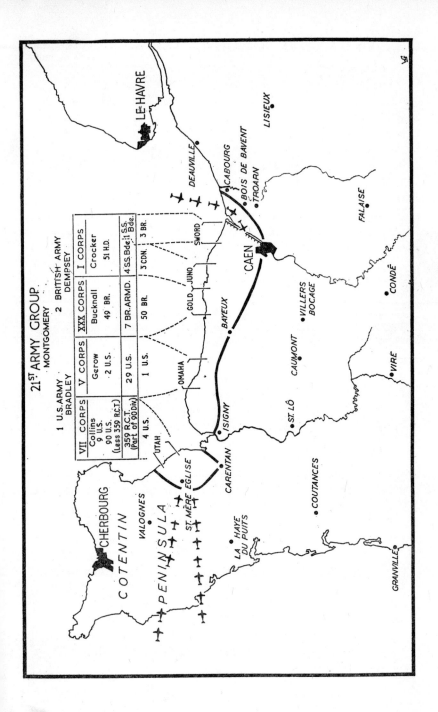

Already, air attacks would have been delivered against the coast-defense batteries. The Fire Plan proper was timed to start on the night preceding the assault when Bomber Command would pick out the ten most important batteries and attack in saturation strength. Medium bombers would then take up the theme on a further six similar targets, the operation due to start soon before first light—the same time as bombardment began from armored assault craft. After this, naval gunfire, directed by spotting aircraft, would join in the assault. The specially fitted craft had withering weapons at their disposal: 4.7-inch guns, 4-inch mortars, barrages of 5-inch rockets, tanks specially fitted with 75-mm. howitzers, 17-pounder antitank guns, as well as ordinary field guns.

And then—half an hour before H-Hour the holocaust from heavy bombers of the 8th U.S. Air Force and medium bombers of the 9th U.S. Air Force. These were timed to go into action against the coast defense artillery and enemy beach localities as late as possible. In fact the whole Joint Fire Plan aimed at building up this barrage to a tremendous crescendo to reach its climax only ten minutes before the first troops waded ashore. Then from H-Hour minus ten minutes the fighters and fighter-bombers would take up the offensive inland. The enemy would have no time at all to recover before the invasion was on.

The strategy took shape at SHAEF where the last two decisions to be made were the actual selection of D-Day and H-Hour—the time the leading assault craft hit the beach. Night was ruled out first of all: it should be daylight, but with a moonlit night for the passage. Daylight was vital for accurate siting of bombardment and also the landing itself. H-Hour had to be as early after first light as possible, to give the enemy least time to notice; and to give the Allies maximum hours of light to consolidate and land the follow-up forces on the second tide before nightfall.

The precise time for H-Hour was fixed by taking into account the period before sunrise when aircraft spotting from high up for naval guns, and heavy bombers, also at a considerable altitude, could see sufficiently—but before the coast defenders at sea level could claim the same. The time required for bombardment from sea and air was whittled down as fine as feasible, the duration decided on eventually being from the first sign of morning light to forty minutes later.

From this, it was settled that H-Hour should be fixed for the moment when the bombardment stopped—forty minutes after first light—and on a day when the tide at this time was three hours before high water. As these conditions could not be obtained on all assault beaches at once, due to the whims of the English Channel, a separate H-Hour for each beach had to be used instead. This meant a compromise, as the Fire Plan could not be divided into separate sectors. Ultimately H-Hour varied from 0630 in the West to 0745 in the East sector.

Time and tide wait. . . .

Finding the right time to coincide with the right tide on a moonlit night eliminated all but three possible dates every month. The target date was still set for May 31, 1944, but a week or so one way or the other was obviously inevitable since so few dates could be considered. After May 31, the next trio of dates offering the vital conditions were June 5, 6, and 7.

Along with Montgomery's main plans went the cover plan designed to point to the Pas de Calais as the goal. Two ideas besides those mentioned earlier were full-scale embarkation signposting in the Dover-Folkestone area, and the aim to keep invasion preparations to proportions which would suggest it was still some six weeks off when it finally happened.

With the cover plan went several diversions to distract the enemy from the Allies' real intentions and area of main assault. These will be noticed at the D-Day stage.

By the end of D-Day, all eight Allied divisions were to be well ashore along with Commandos, Rangers, and fourteen tank regiments. Within a week, basic divisions would have risen to thirteen and by D+20, two dozen divisions would be ashore.

In addition to detailed planning, Montgomery had an over-all date aim and general principles for the troops to adopt to meet this. Sustained energy and drive was paramount. Beachheads had to be linked and then the troops must push on and penetrate inland before opposition crystallized. Leading formations were being told to by-pass major centers of resistance and peg-out claims farther on. Determined leadership must be maintained to retain the initiative of invasion and resist counterattack.

Montgomery was aware of the normal procedure of producing "phase lines" on a map to indicate target positions to be reached by leading troops each few days. A phased map was drawn in April, but he did not feel too happy about the actual lines it bore. Montgomery always had in mind reaching the Seine and the Loire by D+90, but felt that interim estimates would only be misleading and unreal in an operation of this massive magnitude. In fact his Seine-Loire target date was reached on D+75, with a fortnight to spare.

So the planning progressed. Maintaining the 2nd British Army for the first few days might be a headache, so Beach Maintenance Areas came into existence. In the over-all administration and estimates, the weather was expected to be "reasonable" during June, July and August, but plans had to be made against the proverbial rainy day—which more or less coincided with midsummer and might have wrecked the entire invasion.

Montgomery, like Eisenhower, had only a bare five months in England before D-Day, and most of that had to be occupied by planning. But training the troops was just as essential, and most of the forces available for Operation Overlord lacked battle experience. Montgomery saw they got as near the real thing as possible in that spring's training, and traveled all over the country encouraging them by his example.

On April 7 and 8 all the general officers of the Allied armies in the invasion gathered at St. Paul's School to hear Montgomery's planning. Later Churchill also addressed the conference briefly.

Shortly before this, the Premier had told Eisenhower:

"If by the coming winter you have established yourself with your 36 Allied divisions firmly on the Continent and have the Cherbourg and Brittany peninsulas in your grasp, I will proclaim this operation to the world as one of the most successful of the war."

Eisenhower replied: "I assure you that the coming winter will see the Allied forces on the borders of Germany itself."

And so the training went on. On April 2, with only two months to prepare, Lieutenant Colonel Otway received his invasion orders: to take the British 9th Battalion, Parachute Regiment, on the most dangerous mission imaginable, the destruction of the coastal battery near Merville. This vast emplacement was a fantastically formidable proposition. Its guns were said to be 150-mm. caliber mounted in concrete constructions 12 feet high and 5 feet deep. More concrete, earthworks, and steel doors all added to the battery's solidity, while machine guns defended the garrison. Twenty weapon pits appeared on aerial photographs, the whole position being surrounded by a cattle fence, a mine field, and a barbed-wire fence.

Near Newbury, Otway got the sappers to build a scale model of the battery complete with obstacles. Day and night rehearsals continued throughout April and May, more often than not with live ammunition to resemble real life—and death. By the end of May, each one of the thirty-five officers and 600 enlisted men knew precisely his part in the operation. Then there followed an intensive five-day briefing, with every man submitting his own sketch of the position he would occupy. Now at last they reckoned they were ready for Merville.

The final figure for manpower to be moved across the Channel in two days—D-Day and D+1—was 176,000. Behind those were the supply forces and staffs in England, while carrying the forces to France were the crews of some 5,000 ships and craft.

Five thousand vessels.

This was what Admiral Sir Bertram Ramsay had under his command. And taking part in the whole operation would be no less than two million men. Summarized, Ramsay had to break the strong crust of coast defenses by bombardment as well as land the Allied fighting forces, and secondly, to continue their reinforcement without a pause for five or six weeks. The organization involved need not be stressed.

But before the day came exercises on a large scale. These were vital to many of the assault forces, yet the danger existed of the Germans discovering them and attacking the vulnerable craft involved in such an operation. Luckily all rehearsals prior to exercise Tiger escaped any enemy notice. Tiger, however, was a

tragedy. The exercise involved an American assault force, a formation comprising the western flank of the U.S. area, the Utah beach.
U for Utah. With its assembly ports of Torbay, Brixham, Dartmouth and Salcombe, this was part of the designated Western
Task Force, and on the night of April 27-28 was exercising in
Lyme Bay when three groups of fast-moving German E-boats
penetrated the patrols covering the assault craft. They caught the
last convoy to sail on this exercise, consisting of eight tank-landing
ships, and pressed home a sudden and successful attack. In the
dark waters off Lyme Regis the E-boats sank two of the LSTs and
damaged a third. American assault troops were flung fully laden
into the water, and before the attack could be beaten off, many
of them were drowned. The naval defensive patrols were on the
weak side during this exercise, and if the episode was tragic, it
taught everyone the need for as many protective warships and
craft as could humanly be mustered on D-Day. This was an exercise. The real thing would be worse.

Before the final rehearsals for the other four assault forces were
held came the gradual concentration of troops into their particular
areas. From these, they would move on to marshaling zones and
ultimately be brought forward to the embarkation points. And these
ports reached from Felixstowe to Plymouth and round to South
Wales. Vehicles and equipment had to be waterproofed for landing from craft into the sea short of the beach itself. Rations, French
currency, security, and dozens of other details could not be overlooked. Nor could the possibility of postponement due to weather
be overlooked lest feeding and billeting the advance waves be
chaotic.

Production of certain craft and equipment was still short in early
May, but by now preparations were advanced for exercise Fabius
which was to test the basic embarkation arrangements. This involved actually moving and "shipping" thousands of the forces
who would be repeating the experience in a month's time under
conditions of active service. The exercise was far from inactive,
however, and involved assault forces O, G, J, and S. The first of
these formed the Weymouth, Portland, and Poole contingent of
the American task force and was destined to land on the eastern

flank of the U.S. area on Omaha beach. The other three forces, G, J, and S, were to sail from the Hampshire and Sussex waters, the first two from Southampton, the Solent and Spithead, the third from Portsmouth, Spithead, Newhaven, and Shoreham.

The exercise tested the simultaneous sailing of the three forces based there, and also checked the naval commander in chief's control of all Channel movements. The navy's side of Fabius went well, but a freshening southwesterly wind blew up in the afternoon of the first day: the kind so familiar around all the Island coasts. If the exercise had proceeded according to plan, some of the landing craft would undoubtedly have been damaged, so the program was curtailed. The Allies had not enough for D-Day without losing any in advance of it. By this date, May 4, Allied air superiority had become so strong that the only enemy interference with this substantial rehearsal was an aircraft attack on a destroyer in one of the covering forces.

The same week as Fabius, the various higher headquarters of the invasion forces moved nearer the scene of Operation Overlord. Portsmouth was the nerve center of communications to the main embarkation areas, so a stately home nearby was found for Eisenhower's H.Q., Southwick House. Montgomery and Ramsay were on hand, too, while the Allied Air Force placed its H.Q. in the Stanmore-Uxbridge area.

Then on May 15, the High Command returned to London for a final conference at St. Paul's School. Everyone was there, including H.M. King George VI, Field Marshal Smuts, Churchill, and "generals by the score," as Eisenhower records. Churchill made a much-quoted comment:

"I am hardening on this operation."

This did not mean that he had been opposed to it previously, merely that now he wanted to strike even if the limiting conditions laid down for the invasion were not exactly fulfilled.

Churchill questioned what he considered an excess of motor cars and nonfighting vehicles, and also made a mental note of the staggering number of 2,000 officers and clerks accompanying the invasion to keep records. This reminded him of Admiral Andrew Cunningham's story that dental chairs were actually landed at

Algiers in the first flight of Operation Torch! The figures of vehicles to support Churchill's contention were that by D+20 there would be 902,000 men in Normandy and 189,000 vehicles—one for less than each five men.

Still on the subject of vehicles, Churchill had been endeavoring to include a French division in the invasion, for political reasons as well as sentimental, but this Leclerc division seemed to be short of vehicles. Churchill asked Eisenhower for his help and was assured that deficiencies would be made good from the large American supplies.

Yet another decision, for Ramsay this time, was the actual percentage of available landing craft on which he could count in the operation. Getting and keeping these craft in operational order called for great effort, and Ramsay was reluctant to expect more than about 90 per cent of all craft to be available. In fact, however, the proportion reached the amazing figure of 99.3 per cent for American landing craft and 97.6 for British. Amazing since most of these craft had already been used extensively in training over the previous months.

Two days after the SHAEF conference in London, and with the results of a special photographic survey of underwater obstacles in his hands, Eisenhower decided on June 5 as D-Day, provided that the weather was satisfactory. Given the right time and tide and moon, however, there was still much more needed to make it possible. It had to be a quiet day with little wind, a cloud base above 3,000 feet, cloud maximum five-tenths, and at least three miles' visibility. The chances of getting all this on a specific date were surprisingly slim for June: 13 to 1 against. If June 5 were unfavorable, the next two days would apply. After that there would have to be a delay of a fortnight.

Meanwhile May proceeded in idyllic weather, with a calm Channel sprinkled by quicksilver sunshine. Twice a week throughout the month, the Supreme Commander conferred with his weather men to test their forecasts. On the basis of these predictions, Eisenhower made dummy decisions for or against a supposed invasion a day and a half ahead—the time he would have to come to his final, fateful order. These helped him to acquire the frame of mind needed eventually. And the forecasts also gave him the chance of judging the qualities of the chief meteorologist Group Captain J. M. Stagg of the R.A.F.

Now the suspense started to mount, to catch hold of everyone who already knew the D-Day date which was less than three weeks off. The secret of this date was being well kept, too, just as was the location of the actual assault. The Germans would have given anything to know in May those two facts: Normandy, June 5. As it was, although they reacted slowly to the general preparations apparent all over southern England, they did step up naval activity. Apart from the intrusion on the invasion exercises, on April 29 enemy forces engaged two Canadian destroyers covering a mine-laying operation off Isle de Batz and two Elbing-class destroyers. Each side lost one destroyer in the action. Also during May enemy E-boats roamed more freely in the central English Channel and air reconnaissance revealed more had been moved to Cherbourg and Havre.

Three days after the D-Day decision, the first enemy U-boat was reported in the western Channel. This forced the Admiralty to revise the disposition of some covering forces but by cooperation with Coastal Command reconnaissance and armed aircraft, they managed to counteract possible danger to the armada from underwater attack. Hardly any U-boat activity occurred on the day itself.

Apart from the earlier April and May mine-laying sorties in the Solent and Spithead, the Germans did not penetrate this vital Isle of Wight armada area. Right up to D-Day, however, Ramsay continued to worry over the outcome of any last-minute large-scale mining operation. For six weeks, enemy mine laying had been intensified off the south coast generally, and two new types of mine introduced. These operations involved aircraft on a scale not attempted for over two years, but by not managing to mine the main assembly waters, the Germans lost a great opportunity.

Eight

THE days of May were running out amid a blaze of sun. Eisenhower had little time to admire the grounds of Southwick House, however, and his sole interest in the weather was its effect on the enterprise under his command. Late in the month, Leigh-Mallory was still unhappy about the decision to drop two airborne divisions on the Cherbourg peninsula. He foresaw 50 per cent or higher losses if this part of Overlord was allowed to continue. Eisenhower's expert adviser disagreed with the Air Chief Marshal's pessimism and so it remained to the Supreme Commander alone to decide. Eisenhower went to his tent to think it all out and finally followed the plan as already prepared. He telephoned the news to Leigh-Mallory and then resumed his urgent work once more.

All over England the camps lay pitched. Now a fever began to grip the forces. After a rash of rumors, groups left distant places where they had been stationed all spring, and headed south. Fresh transit camps sprang up; trains tore through the night bearing the men toward their destiny; and tanks, motorcycles, even DUKWs roared down the English roads. Another wait, till at last on May 28, subordinate commanders learned the vital date. From this day on, all who were committed to the invasion were suddenly "sealed" in their ships, their camps, or wherever they were. No one came or went; no mail passed in or out; barbed wire stretched all around like concentration camps.

Southern England was one vast camp, crowded with forces and crushed with equipment. Every encampment, barracks, vehicle park and unit, was precisely charted on master maps. Their schedule for movement had been so wonderfully worked out that each unit would reach its vessels at the exact time they were ready. As the last day of May dawned, "the whole mighty host was tense as a coiled spring," as Eisenhower says, just waiting to be sped across the Channel in the greatest amphibious assault in history. Now the briefing was over. All knew from maps and photos the beach they would assault. Officers had even earmarked houses near Caen for their platoon headquarters! The men relinquished all their personal possessions and donned new antivermin battle dress. From camps to transit areas, the men were soon to be moved in boatloads.

Before June and D-Day, Winston Churchill wanted it assured that he would be able to watch the pre-H-Hour bombardment from a suitable escort cruiser. Ramsay drew up a plan for this, but felt bound to tell Eisenhower, who could not countenance such an unjustified risk. And when Churchill took his weekly luncheon with the King on Tuesday, May 30, he was asked where he would be on D-Day. When Churchill told the King, His Majesty expressed a similar wish. The next day, however, George VI wrote to the Prime Minister explaining that on reflection it would not be proper for either of them to be there. After a further exchange of letters, Churchill reluctantly agreed.

Now the number one question was the weather. In May, more than half the days would have been good enough for Eisenhower to launch the liberation. But ironically Thursday, June 1, dawned a dull, difficult day. The tents pitched all over the southern counties cast no shadow as the day passed. Stagg found the whole situation marginal. No foolproof forecast could be made with these conflicting indications. From June 1 onward, the Supreme Commander held meetings twice a day solely to consider the weather reports. These were not held at conventional times, but at 9:30 P.M. and 4 A.M. Four in the morning at Southwick House. Hampshire villages slept all around in the hush before dawn— Hambledon, Fareham, Southwick, Wickham, and over Portsdown Hill, the old castle town of Porchester. Then beyond it, Portsmouth Harbor and the Solent crowded with craft, with the muted outline of the Isle of Wight rising from the sea, a blurred etched line against the southern sky. Only the sound of the power station and the creak of cranes in the dockyard disturbed the night.

The Anglo-American committee, headed by Group Captain Stagg, examined and analyzed every scrap of meteorological information which poured into the house from many sources. To help the forecasts further, two U.S. and two British warships were stationed specially in the Atlantic to transmit reports of the weather which would be likely to head in the prevailing westerly way toward England, the Channel and Normandy. They had already gained extra experience from a similar service for the Fabius exercise.

Many things were already happening elsewhere, ships actually on the move, but in the final analysis, it was Eisenhower's decision when to launch the assault which would affect them all. The Gooseberries, for instance. Consider Lieutenant Commander J. E. Taylor, R.N.R., aboard the liner *Durban,* one of the 60 blockships soon due to be scuttled off the Arromanches beaches. How long ago was it since he had attended that first meeting at the Gooseberry H.Q. near the Mall?—when he had heard for the very first time of all those mysterious Mulberries and Gooseberries; Corncobs, Phoenix, Whales and Bombardons; Spud Pierhead, Beetles and Baker Dolphins.

"Mulberry A—American—at St. Laurent," he heard, "and Mulberry B—British—at Arromanches." But the breakwaters would not be enough alone, so—

"There'll be five Gooseberries, one at Varreville, off St. Laurent, Arromanches, Courseulles, and Ouistreham." The Gooseberry shelters were to be formed mainly by merchant ships which would proceed under their own steam to the offshore sites. Four warships were among the final choice.

Taylor remembered, too, Rear Admiral Mulberry/Pluto showing him a map bearing a small printed card:

"This project is so vital to the success of Overlord that it might be described as the crux of the whole operation."

Rather a frightening thought. Frightening, too, was the model room at H.Q. with its sandy scale-model of the Normandy beaches. Just a small affair, but discovered by the wrong person it would have ruined the whole invasion. London was full of secrets like that just now.

Taylor went north and met a Vernon equipment officer who was in charge of wiring and fitting all the scuttling charges in a dozen of the 60 ships scattered among out-of-the-way ports up to 40 miles apart.

Passing Wigtown Bay, he saw signs of the Mulberry project first-hand. A dredger was lowering great stilts or "spuds" onto the bottom of the bay. There in the quiet of Wigtown Bay, the first pierhead, its spuds firmly planted on the sea bed, rose and fell magically with every tide.

Taylor recalled how the plans for assembling and sailing the blockships had slowly emerged. Two waiting ports were chosen —Methil and Oban—and as the ships' conversions were completed and their charge machinery all installed they sailed to one or other of these two ports—and waited. The dozen which the Vernon officer had prepared were already nearby, so needed only a short trip. Taylor's own ship sailed from Portsmouth in May. In the early light of a spring morning, the liner *Durban* weighed anchor and the faded elegance of her slim lines vanished into the Channel mist, followed ponderously by a less sleek ship, the *Sumatra*. It was past mid-May now, and while Eisenhower was starting his "dummy runs" on weather forecasting, these two dissimilar ships followed the coast up to Oban. At Loch Linnhe, they found a score of other blockships waiting for them. All bore three-figure numbers on both port and starboard sides, and the arrival of *Durban* and *Sumatra* with matching markings created a ripple of anticipation in the peaceful port. It would not be long now.

Taylor climbed to a clifftop house overlooking the Firth of Lorne and looked down at the harbor with its twenty-two old ships clustered cozily below. Two days later they sailed around from Oban to Methil.

May 26. D−10 by the original reckoning. The order came: "Convoy will weigh anchor in succession."

Out to sea, the anti-aircraft gun crews exercised, while four minesweepers on the port quarter plied a course calculated to clear a way through an imaginary mine field. Night, and the light of Kinnaird Head flashing regularly. Something to catch hold of in the enveloping dark. Earlier someone reported sighting a submarine periscope off Duncansly Head. The northern edge of Scotland crawled past, and Cape Wrath in night again, rounded in relentless rain. Through it all the stuttering engines of the ancient ships kept turning, and they were back at Oban again.

D−7 now. Duffle coats were issued for the following week, as many of the men would be on an upper deck of another vessel or open landing craft once the blockships were sunk. Duffle coats would be their bedding, and the weather was already getting worse. The issue included a first-aid pack, 48 hours' emergency rations, knife, fork, spoon, tin plate, mug, and toilet paper—plus a life belt, gas mask, steel helmet, identity disk, and pay book.

Then as June came in, the ships went out. And with the *Durban* in her wardroom went bluebells, primroses and rhododendron blossoms gathered from the hillsides of the Scottish coast. Flowers which would live for a week and find a strange grave to adorn. Strange and sad, yet splendid too.

The naval officer in charge sailed in *Sumatra* as the entire sixty vessels headed for the Bristol Channel. They made a remarkable convoy in three groups, with twenty-two British and Allied ships in front, sixteen American in the middle, and the remainder in the rear.

"Speed five knots—keep closed up," said the flags flying on the *Alynbank*.

A magnificent motley of vessels whose logical end would be a breaker's yard—not the most decisive naval action of the war! With the evening came rain, and a count revealing all present. But gathering darkness brought trouble, too. *Dover Hill* and *Empire Tamar* stopped and turned athwart and finally recovered. Then *Empire Defiance* had to be taken in tow: a frantic seven hours' work in her engine room followed until the condenser trouble causing her breakdown was at last cured. It was clearly going to be all the ships could do to get to their destination. At daylight they were joined by two American concrete ships. Then the moon came out, broken by ragged clouds across it, suggesting an end of fine weather. Land's End by morning and round into the English Channel.

They had two sealed operational orders on board, giving the date and time of D-Day and H-Hour. One was Serial 10 and the other Serial 1.

Serial 10 meant June 5, 0640. Serial 1 was June 6, 0720.

Which would it be? A good question, and the only man in the world who could know the answer when the time came was Eisenhower.

Friday, June 2. A day of suspense with the weather still sluggish. The outlook for D-Day, then Monday, June 5, was about the same as for Saturday and Sunday. In the evening, the first warships sailed from Scapa, Belfast and the Clyde and down through the Irish Sea. Today, too, the two midget submarines charged with the task of marking the assault areas for the first craft set sail from Portsmouth Harbor, or more accurately Fort Blockhouse.

Five men could be accommodated in both X.20 and X.23, the same submarines which had carried out the beach reconnaissance off the Arromanches sector earlier in the year. In addition to the commanding officer and first lieutenant, they carried an engine room artificer and two COPPs—Combined Operations Pilotage Parties.

All morning and afternoon of June 2, the two little craft could scarcely be seen for activity around them. The mass of gear for the operation had to be stowed, compactly, in the special stowing bags designed for it. Twelve Luftwaffe bottles were stuck down the main hatch to guarantee an extra day's supply of oxygen in addition to the craft's ordinary built-in cylinders in case of accidents. Into the small space below went three R.A.F. rubber dinghies, two small portable radar beacons, some Sten guns, lightweight diving suits, three flashing lamps with batteries and 18-foot telescopic masts. Along with all this general and special marking gear revolvers and ammunition were included too.

This was all carried inboard. Outside, extra buoyancy chambers had been built while two small special anchors were stowed for'ard, bollards incorporated fore and aft, and an 18-foot sounding pole had been secured on as well. Into the hull went an echo-sounder, while an upper-deck repeater was rigged from the master gyro-compass. Each vessel was, in fact, a floating store. The COPPs' first job was to make certain of the crafts' navigation, as an accurate position was the crux of the initial impact of the invasion. All this preparation went on while the dumpy little ferry boats from Portsmouth to Gosport steamed within a few yards of the X-crafts' berths at Blockhouse.

At half-past nine on Friday evening, June 2, X.20 and X.23 slipped silently from their moorings and set course to make the East Gate in the Portsmouth boom.

Operation Gambit was on.

Past the gray stone walls of old Portsmouth, glinting gold in a fitful sunset, they moved at slow speed. The weathered red brick of Blockhouse faded from view and three-quarters of an hour later the two tiny craft passed through the boom gate, a reminder of defense against attackers and invaders in another war, and met their escorts.

Now night fell with clouds rolling in from the west. X.23 was astern of H.M.S. *Sapper* and the two found it hard to join company. An awkward swell lifted and lowered the tiny craft and it took another three-quarters of an hour to pass the tow. Communications were sufficiently bad, in fact, that the craft stayed on the surface so that all signals could be made visually. Yet in spite of the sea, a steady speed was being maintained. X.20 followed, and the two teams kept informal company.

Lieutenant Ken Hudspeth was commanding X.20, and Lieutenant George Honour, X.23: both R.N.V.R. officers. No snags developed until early Saturday morning, when the little fleet had to stop to allow Hudspeth to clear a dan-buoy mooring wire which had fouled X.20's idle screw. Just before dawn the time approached for the two midgets to be left alone. Their two escort trawlers flashed final signals with subdued lights. Last-minute checks were made.

"Good luck" messages flashed from each large ship to its tiny ward. Then the X-craft slipped their tows and parted from their escorts—and from each other. They were really on their own now. Five men in each, with a load of responsibility.

Honour's voice came crackling, distorted over the phones, from the wet and cheerless casing up aloft:

"Full ahead main engine, course 172 degrees."

As the early light lanced the sea, they dived to avoid any chance of being spotted. They caught a trim and kept to a steady 30-foot depth, half speed ahead on the main motor. On and on exactly like this for the whole day of Saturday, June 3, and the same course of 172. Honour hoped to reach the French coast without using any of his precious oxygen, and to do this he had to raise the induction once every five hours and run the engine for a few minutes to draw a fresh air supply through the boat.

With the later hours of evening, the boat had been ventilated three times without breaking surface. Then as soon as darkness fell, the craft came up to the surface to charge the batteries, while the same course was continued.

Sunday, June 4, three o'clock in the morning, and the speed went up to full ahead. Another hour and a dead reckoning placed the craft quite near its final position. Nothing now remained except to wait for morning when some accurate periscope navigation could be executed. So the main ballast tanks were slowly flooded and X.23 settled happily on the bottom. Four of the five aboard slept soundly for four hours till about 0800. Then came a quick breakfast, a few pints of water pumped out of the compensating tank, and a slow rise to periscope depth.

It took only a minute or two to ascertain that they were the right distance offshore. Through the day periscope, Honour saw a bare and flat coast line, rather like East Anglia except for an absence of creeks and inlets. Trees were few, and no semblance of a cliff seemed to be visible. But away to port there was a river mouth, or what looked like one, and a couple of church spires pointing heavenward on this early Sabbath morning. Could they have landed dead on position, just off the estuary of the Orne? It seemed too good to be true.

"Course due east; 650 revs. Keep her at periscope depth."

Honour peered through the periscope continually, and soon

74

determined that they were indeed off the Orne. They were able to identify both the churches which stood exactly where the map marked them, while a cross-bearing on another conspicuous eminence fixed the position beyond doubt. A hum of excitement hung in the air of the submarine.

Honour kept her at periscope depth, or just below, until 1100, taking periodic peeps at the land. But there was nothing at all to be seen.

"Complete picnic," he announced.

But they still had to wait. At teatime they rose to periscope depth again and confirmed their position by fresh fixes. Then they bottomed for a few more hours. Silence, supper, sleep, games of liar dice, just off the invasion coast!

A last check over the equipment. Next day was due to be D-Day. Only a matter of hours now. Promptly at 2315, after the last summer light had dropped west, they surfaced and switched on their checked and rechecked radio receiver. The right wavelength, the right program, the right time. But no message yet. They'd know that within a few minutes. The weather was bad. The invasion might be on—or it might not.

Nine

SATURDAY, June 3, and precious little encouragement in the weather. A westerly wind was blowing inland, past the Needles and all along the Solent, whipping up its waters and rocking the clustered landing craft. Heavy cloud was due to drop still lower and the outlook for Monday, D-Day, was not good. Two of the stations from which forecasts were forthcoming gave completely opposite versions of what was likely to develop! Scarcely the sort of start Eisenhower wanted.

He still had until the early hours of Sunday to decide. Meanwhile, Churchill drove down to Portsmouth with Ernest Bevin and Field Marshal Smuts and saw some of the troops embarking for Normandy. Stokes Bay, peaceful peacetime haunt of Gosport people for bathing and beach picnics, was a mass of barbed wire and landing craft. Churchill visited one of the headquarters ships and then sailed down the Solent, boarding one ship after another and meeting the men.

Elsewhere the loading went on. In the harbors all round the coast, the infantry and tank-landing craft lay six deep out from the jetty. Everything was covered with camouflage netting to prevent recognition from the air as they lay six deep for as far as the eye could see. LCT 7008, L.C.H. 317, U 23—they all had a magic meaning in the stupendous scheme about to begin.

Then the troops, split into boatloads, saw their craft for the first time. Loudspeakers told them which one was theirs, and they humped their kit on a bent back and marched across wired-off promenades and beaches to the boats. Down the gangways, often with folding bicycles—if they were Commandos. And the armor went aboard as well. Cranes dangled great lorries over the gap between wharf and ship, then swung them aboard, camouflage roofs and all. The jaws of a tank-landing ship opened beside the quay and a Sherman tank, gun pointing menacingly, nosed aboard. Others drove directly on from beaches, up the special ramps.

GIs filed singly over the sand of a west-of-England shore, their tin hats snug on their heads, ready for action.

"Why are we waiting?" sang a boatload of British.

Back to Portsmouth, and carrier crews waited about on board beside their supplies.

RETURN EMPTY TO R.A.S.C., was marked one sack of something. They would be lucky. But probably it would be back at the Hilsea depot within a few days. Strange to think. Life did not just stop once D-Day dawned. It would go on and there must be supplies. In the background stood the tall landmark of Vernon mining tank and the power station chimneys.

All along the coast the fantastic Phoenix creations were taking final form. And until wanted, they sat on the bed of the sea, which had to be perfectly flat and shallow. The Phoenixes, as Admiral Tennant said, looked as if "someone had picked up Chicago and put it down on the Sussex foreshore."

Extra parking areas were found for about five miles of pier roadway at Peel Bank and Marchwood, opposite Southampton, so that with towering pierheads suggesting some factory risen from the water, the scene in the Solent was equally bizarre!

But strangely enough, days passed without Von Runstedt even receiving a report of this amassed armada. Neither was Ramsay's H.Q. of Southwick House detected from the air. There was parkland surrounding the Georgian residence and security went to great lengths to keep it secret. No one had been allowed to walk in the fields, as trodden grass would have been revealed in aerial photographs.

In the library—also Ramsay's mess—that Saturday evening Eisenhower again met his meteorologists. Stagg was far from happy now. Admiral Creasy called him "six feet two of Stagg, and six feet one of gloom." A high-pressure area over the Azores was giving way, and three depressions seemed to be headed up the Channel.

His four-day forecast, embracing all three possible dates, spoke of high winds, low clouds and even fog.

Postponement seemed more than likely, but as Eisenhower knew he must launch his attack on the first possible day, June 5, he decided that Force U and Force O should sail from Devonshire and Portland as planned originally. He could wait no longer if they were to meet their schedule for June 5. He hoped there might be a sudden switch, but Stagg found the conflicting reports from the weather ships and stations the most uncertain of the whole year. It was rotten luck right at the start.

The evening meeting started at 2100 and lasted until after midnight. When they all reassembled at 0400 on Sunday, June 4, it was within two hours of the main assault force's scheduled sailing. Stagg now had to quote rising winds and low clouds. Ironically, as Ramsay looked out just before the meeting began, the sky seemed clear and the wind low! But Stagg was adamant. Waves would be high, air support almost impossible, naval support bombardment inefficient, and the whole operation highly hazardous—as it would be even in fine weather. And so, although Montgomery would have agreed to go ahead, the difficulty of air support forced the Supreme Commander to postpone D-Day for twenty-four hours.

One decision, and another one to be made within a day.

All Force U was at sea by now, and part of Force O. Orders went out within minutes to tell them to reverse and return to harbor. Instructions for this emergency were already worked out, of course, but it was not easy. Force U2A failed to receive the recall signal. This was a large and slow assault convoy composed of 128 tank-landing craft with their escorts. By 0900 on Sunday the force was 25 miles south of St. Catherine's Point, Isle of Wight, and still steering due south. Two destroyers raced out of the Portsmouth assembly area with a Walrus aircraft overhead to intercept it, otherwise the force would before long have been detected by enemy radar, if not reconnaissance.

Force U ran into rough sea on their return, and although the whole force was ordered back into Weymouth Bay, some never reached it and were still punching toward it when the next decision was due. Throughout June 4, too, doubt arose whether Force U would be fit to go ahead without returning to re-form. This would almost certainly have meant putting off D-Day for a fortnight, so Eisenhower heard with relief that Rear Admiral Kirk was ready to proceed.

The other ships already on the move found the stormy Irish Sea difficult for maneuver, yet somehow they managed to regain port, refuel, and be ready to resume operations a day later. A silent but brilliant service.

So no harm was done to D-Day. And as the false starters staggered back for the gun again, other second-line forces were still surging to the south coast by road and rail.

"Home, home on the range," wafted over Portsea Bridge as a truckload rumbled across. "Where seldom is heard a discouraging word. . . ." Some would never see home any more. They had two days to live.

The armada lay uneasily at anchor, as the troops passed the time. They smeared grease on their faces for camouflage, and then waited for the word.

Over in Operations Room at Southwick House, the whole picture was seen spread on the wall. A long, lofty room, here was the very heart of Operation Neptune, as the actual sea aspect of Overlord was called. In the room were usually about forty people, mostly naval officers or Wrens plotting positions on charts and attending to the stream of signals borne in by an endless belt appearing through a hole in the wall from the cipher office. Air liaison officers, military liaison, and American staff officers made up most of the remainder.

The walls of this high room were papered in white and gold, and at one end the wall was covered by an enormous blackboard chart of the Channel. Up and down in front of this moved a traveling stepladder, used by the Wrens progressively more and more for plotting on the map the hour-to-hour position of all units at sea—or base.

In front of the big blackboard wall map, and to one side, sat the signal officer. Level with him, but near the center of the room, sat Rear Admiral George Creasy, Chief of Staff to the Naval C in C, Admiral Ramsay. These two desks marked a line across the room about four yards from the wall map. That space was the "holy of holies," reserved for Ramsay and his immediate staff. And there the C in C spent many long hours—particularly after the assault began.

But now it was still only Sunday, June 4. When Stagg awoke at 1000 that morning after advising a postponement, he was surprised to see a sky almost bright and only a light wind, but by 1100 the Admiralty had issued a gale warning to all shipping in the Irish Sea. The weather forecast seemed to be on its way. But would the clearer conditions coming from the east American coast reach here in time?

Churchill and Smuts had returned to London by train at a late hour the previous night, and the Prime Minister did not get to bed until half past one. Yet by five thirty he was awake, and had sent for General Ismay to hear for certain of the postponement. Now he was waiting again.

So Sunday passed somehow. The storm gathered and grew, and a strong west wind sent vicious breakers rolling up Channel. Many of the men herded in small landing craft, unused to the sea, were taking their antisickness pills before the craft weighed anchor. A day in a craft in these conditions can seem eternity, to the stomach and nerves. So the squat craft rode out the storm somehow, while the wind tore at the silver-gray barrage balloons overhead—protection against enemy air activity which fortunately could not possibly exist today.

The wind and the rain reached the panes of Southwick House, too, rattling the window frames in staccato sounds. Eisenhower ate an evening meal and then moved into the library for the 2100 weather conference. Everyone was there: Eisenhower, Montgomery, Tedder, Smith, Ramsay, Leigh-Mallory, and others. Yet it did not look like one of the most momentous meetings in history. They sat easily in a casual group of armchairs and leather sofas, their notes in buff files. One and all knew what was at stake: before dawn the decision had to be made. Now or never. Or at least not for a fortnight, with all the reaction and upheaval entailed. And keeping security for that additional time seemed too much to expect. In fact, so complex was the organization that it really could not be put into reverse. After briefing, embarkation, and all the personal tension attached to it. And the Russians were timing their offensive to coincide with the Western invasion.

Eisenhower presided and asked Stagg for his prognosis. Stagg reported a depression over Portsmouth, to be followed by fair conditions: 5/10ths cloud, 2000-3000 feet base, lower wind, lasting until Tuesday morning. Then the cloud would increase to 8/10ths to 10/10ths followed by variable skies. The general inference was disturbed, but Stagg hoped for some improvement.

Leigh-Mallory queried whether this agreed with the R.A.F. weather men. Stagg said that it did. There would be almost perfect visual bombing weather from Monday evening to early forenoon Tuesday. Then good and poor periods from Tuesday afternoon till Friday.

Although they were all lounging, the discussion was dramatic as Ramsay observed that Admiral Kirk must be told within the next half hour if Overlord were to take place on Tuesday. Amid all the storm and stress and wind and rain, this break in the weather seemed to be a "break" in every sense of the word.

"It's a helluva gamble but it's the best possible gamble," said American Bedell Smith in a picturesque martial phrase.

Leigh-Mallory wondered whether the heavy bombers might find the conditions prejudiced by low cloud on their second mission—if not the first. But Eisenhower countered by pointing out the force of fighter-bombers the Allies had on call. Turning to Montgomery, Eisenhower asked:

"Do you see any reason for not going on Tuesday?"

Monty replied: "I would say—go!"

Ramsay also agreed.

Eisenhower went on: "The alternatives are too chancy. The question is—just how long can you hang this operation on the end of a limb and let it hang there?"

The decision became increasingly clear cut as each hour passed. For now it was no longer possible to consider Wednesday, the seventh, as some of the warships and convoys already at sea would not have enough fuel to last till then, nor time to put into port for fresh supplies. Thursday would be too late for the second high tide to occur before darkness.

"Well, boys, there it is," Eisenhower concluded. "I don't see how we can possibly do anything else. I'm quite positive we must give the order. The only question is whether we should meet again in the morning."

As the air program still seemed doubtful, he decided to defer the final order, but he had to let Ramsay go ahead with the early warnings to the Americans, who needed the time to traverse the extra distance from the West Country waters, where they were unhappily anchored after the false alarm of the previous day.

Around midnight the meeting adjourned for four hours. Eisenhower ran into Stagg, waiting outside the library, and begged him not to change the forecast during the next few hours! Then Eisenhower hurried into his staff car through heavy rain to return to his own camp a mile away from Southwick House for a bit of rest.

At 0330 he was up again to feel the camp "shaking and shuddering" with the wind. Making the return trip by car, the rain slashed the windshield head-on, and the wheels slipped in the mud of the makeshift road.

The final meeting climaxing all its forerunners, real and rehearsed, lasted from 0400 to 0430. It seemed surprising to be even considering invasion with the weather still so stormy, let alone having half-committed themselves to it already. Stagg said that the adverse conditions predicted previously for the French coast at dawn, June 5, were actually operating there now, which was in one way a relief—to know that these had been avoided. And even as he spoke, the sky was starting to clear a little, and the rain which had greeted Eisenhower earlier eased steadily. The only change since the last forecast was for the better, Stagg was glad to be able to reveal, and the fair interval clearing southern England at that time would probably last well over twenty-four hours and into Tuesday afternoon. The long-term outlook was still not all that might be desired, but the good period came as a blessing out of the blue—or rather the gray of the preceding days. Eisenhower balanced the danger of delay for a fortnight against the

83

later bad weather stopping the build-up forces. But despite all this, as soon as Stagg finished speaking, an air of relief spread round the room. Tedder and others asked one or two questions, and then Stagg and his men left the library to allow the commanders to make the decision.

Leigh-Mallory still thought that air conditions would be below the planned acceptable minimum, but realized that this applied equally to the enemy. So even the cautious R.A.F. commander agreed that there was no other course. Airborne operations would be practicable, anyway; that was vital.

Eisenhower cocked his head to one side in a characteristic way while hearing their last comments, then said quietly but confidently:

"O.K. We'll go."

Five hours earlier, X.23, the midget submarine off Normandy, had surfaced and was waiting for the word. It was to be a coded radio message mixed up in an innocent broadcast, and without it they could not know whether or not the whole procession of landing craft and its accompanying bombardment was due at dawn. George Honour gave his quiet helm-and-speed orders to get her back to the waiting position. But his quiet voice belied the inevitable excitement all of them felt.

Looking at the coast, they could see enemy aircraft landing not far inshore. The airfield must have been dead abeam. More useful still, a fixed red light burned above the entrance to the Orne River, which they had located earlier. A hospitable aid to navigation, Honour thought.

With their position confirmed from soundings, the shore light, and previous fixes, they commenced the final run-in, measuring the distance with the taut-wire gear. Very close in to the enemy shore, they let go the special anchor, which held first time. As the cable was made fast on the for'ard bollards, the time was nearly midnight. Still the suspense about the whole operation held.

June 5, 0055. At last, after an hour's waiting, they received a faint wireless message about the twenty-four hours' postponement.

Honour: "Weigh anchor—slow ahead—course 010."

Monday much the same as Sunday. The tension eased as X.23

sank to the bottom for twelve hours. They slept and even found time to be a bit bored. But gradually the day passed and their excitement returned.

So the twenty-four hours elapsed since they surfaced before, and the log read:

> 2315. Surfaced and commenced wireless watch. Message received operation taking place, but reception was very difficult and master gyro had to be stopped during the period the message was coming in. This unsettled the compass and caused it to be unreliable. However, during the period of wireless watch the craft had already reached and anchored in her marking position, so the compass defection did not prove as serious as it might have done.

Soon after midnight, Honour was able to have the craft flooded down below the surface, to remove any risk of last-minute spotting. Then at 0445, June 6, D-Day, she came slowly back "up top." In a few minutes they had rigged the telescopic mast, made all connections, and the signal light—screened from the shore—was flashing away to sea. X.20 was in her correct position, too, having had the same experience. Each craft had spent 64 hours out of their 76 submerged. Now they sat on the surface, sitting targets, as beacons beckoning the invasion fleet inshore. But all was still quiet, uncannily so. Any minute now, and D-Day would be on, guided by the two tiny craft.

Ten

D−1 and sunrise silhouetted the three thousand landing craft and five hundred warships as they started out to sea. Some were already on their way. Force U for Utah, O for Omaha, and Force G for Gold, from the West. Force J for Juno from the Portsmouth area. And Force S from east of Portsmouth. From Falmouth, Fowey, Plymouth, Salcombe, Dartmouth, Brixham, Torbay, Portland, Weymouth, Poole, Southampton, Solent, Spithead, Shoreham, Newhaven, Harwich and the Nore. All with one purpose: to liberate Europe.

But first came the Channel. Still the wind gusted and whipped the waves to five feet and more. Men gripped their stomachs, gritted their teeth. Guts to be killed was one thing: seasickness another. The wind stood at WSW with a force of 16 to 20 m.p.h. It decreased at times, but then the gusts returned.

The red crosses of a field ambulance unit brought reality to a scene described by Ramsay as unreal through the absence of enemy activity. Someone would need these on the next day. Meanwhile the barrage balloons fluttered over the convoys. Tank-landing craft plowed a line-astern course escorted by a bevy of larger ships.

From the west, north and east they sailed, all through that morning. The first goal? Area Z. This was a circular zone eight miles in diameter and twenty-five miles south of Portsmouth and Hayling Island arranged for rendezvous. From here on, they would follow one of ten swept channels in a southerly direction. Area Z at once became christened Piccadilly Circus by the whole navy, while the army occupied itself by playing cards in the cramped craft or polishing, not their dress, but their French from phrase books. It might come in useful, one way or another. . . .

So that the northern ends, or the start, of the ten approach channels should be precisely positioned, ten special buoys had been laid by three motor launches of Force J at the dead of the night, May 31–June 1. These buoys were timed to transmit signals between 1400 and 2200 on six successive days from June 4. In the afternoon of June 5, ten motor launches took up position to point the buoys for the following forces, and the system proved to be completely successful. A large number of ships, too, were fitted with receivers to obtain positions from the Gee and Decca radio navigational systems, so accuracy of course was never in doubt. And as the ships assembled at Z, the men ate stew followed by plum pudding. And the flat-bottomed tank-landing craft pitched and rolled to the tide.

After lunch began the biggest, most majestic minesweeping operation of the war. For weeks now, numbers of sweepers had been sailing home from the Mediterranean, where they helped pave the way for the Sicily and Italy invasions. From northern and east coast bases they sailed in good time to be, as usual, the vessels in the van of any operation through dangerous waters.

As many as three hundred sweepers moved south in perfect order. Twelve flotillas of large fleet sweepers and many more smaller ones literally swept before them in a broad twelve-channel front, fifteen miles wide at the start and thirty miles at the southern end. These sweepers had had little preliminary practice for such a specialized and important operation, and they also had the extra burden of having to change sweeps during the passage in order to avoid sweeping with an unfavorable tide. Some flotillas had no time to rehearse this tricky maneuver at all, yet it all turned out well on the day.

In their correct formations, and at the moderate speed required for effective sweeping, the ships headed straight toward enemy guns not yet silenced by any naval or air attack. Danger from the air, from E-boats; and U-boats was always present, too. This applied equally to all the armada, but the crews of those who could move with more freedom and take effective evasive action if at-

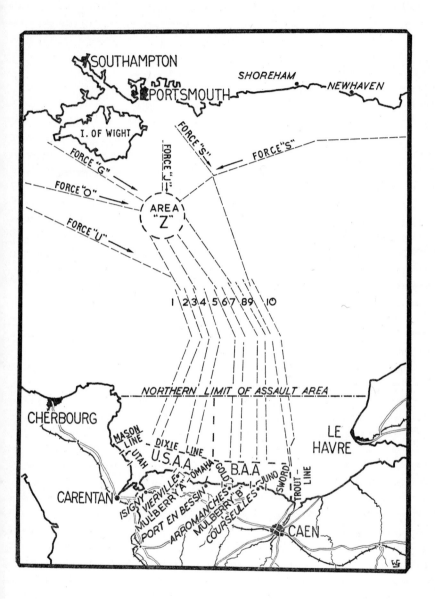

tacked found this magnificent maneuver inspiring. The crews of destroyers, corvettes, and others watched fascinated as the groups of sweepers moved back and forth down the vital channels. Cold-blooded courage accompanied the crews of the sweepers, and the periodic punctuation—or underlining—of their purpose by vicious, violent explosions seemed detached from the peaceful pattern of ships on sea, and an impertinence to their progress!

Hazardous as this was—both from vulnerability to attack and the deathly danger of the mines—the sweepers found fewer fields than they expected. There was reason to think that the Germans would have laid a line right across from the Cherbourg peninsula to Le Havre, but this did not materialize. The credit for foiling the enemy's intention was due to the air forces who had—without knowing it!—delayed the arrival of the mine supplies by their blanket bombing of French railways, and also to the navy. When the mines finally reached Le Havre, the Royal Navy and Coastal Command intercepted the flotilla sent specially from Brest to lay the mines, and dealt with all except one of them.

Thus as the sweepers encountered less interruption than anticipated, they went ahead of schedule and actually were within sight of the invasion coast long before dark. Two flotillas were level with Le Havre by sunset, and so close inshore that some of them could see individual houses on the Vierville coast, where the Omaha landings were to take place in less than twelve hours. Yet for some inexplicable reason, no guns fired on them, so they could not have been seen. Although the Germans were prepared for invasion, they had discounted this week in view of the weather. Yet this lack of identification still seemed amazing. In any case, even if they were spotted, General Richter did not hear of it in Caen! On this day of all others, the German air force flew only a single reconnaissance mission in the West—and this was far from the invasion scene, off the Dutch coast line with its dikes and dunes! Eisenhower could hardly have hoped for such luck!

Yet it was not all due to luck. While the fleet was still assembled at Area Z, the elaborate cover plan, Operation Fortitude, had gone into motion. For five days now, the Allied air forces had been hammering the French coast apparently indiscriminately from Cap

Gris Nez to Le Havre. Even up to D−1 twice the bomb load was being dropped in the Pas de Calais area as on the actual invasion beaches. No doubt now that this deceptive bombing had done its job of diversion wonderfully, so that by quite late on D−1 the enemy had no idea of imminent invasion, or if they had, thought all signs pointed to the Pas de Calais. To underline this, dummy paratroops were dropped in three main areas to cause confusion as to the real destination of our airborne forces soon to be on French soil.

But the main diversions were across the sea near the Straits of Dover. The Allies wanted to conceal the ultimate direction of the fleet moving mainly eastward up the Channel. This force would not reach Area Z till dark, when its change of direction south would not be noticed. This was accomplished by an amazing radar operation designed to deceive the enemy into believing the assault to be aimed farther east. The twofold task was first, to jam enemy warning stations in the actual area to be invaded—Cherbourg to Le Havre—and mislead the Le Havre to Calais stations into reporting the fleet sailing toward their sector.

Thirty-four small ships and over a hundred aircraft undertook this strange mission. Following in the wake of the minesweepers, the vessels aimed for Cap d'Antifer, north of Le Havre, towing as many barrage balloons as they could to simulate big ships on enemy radar screens. Then when they were within radar range they sailed slowly up toward Calais. Overhead, Bomber Command then flew round and round, dropping tinfoil by the bundle to give the Germans false radar readings. The aircraft made endless orbits, slowly drawing nearer the coast, to suggest a convoy of big ships sailing across the Channel to the north of the actual D-Day beaches. Similar diversions off Boulogne also helped toward the eventual state of surprise achieved. What with a phantom fleet off Dover, craft ostensibly sailing on obscure courses up the Channel, dummy paratroops, and jamming on radar sets, the confusion was complete before the end of D−1.

As soon as the sun set on D−1, too, cooperation came with the French Resistance. Arms and equipment had been delivered to them by air for a long time now, and a network of wireless communications operated over a wide area. Agents in the Special Air

91

Service found themselves being flown in unescorted aircraft, lone in the night, to be parachuted down through the dark to blow up strategic points—alone or acting with the Resistance. Already our bombs had torn a line of destruction in the roads and rails leading to Normandy. Their job was to get at the inaccessible vital places. No massive raid with a smoky pall of death as its aftermath. Theirs was the silent strike, then the explosion, and escape if they were lucky.

All the day of D—1, the armada assembled. The only sound of war yet, the deep, dramatic eruption of depth charges from H.M.S. *Holmes,* after the possible presence of a U-boat was reported. Then the spray settled, and only the waves and wind spoiled the scene. Spaced out to avoid attack on more than one, the ships slowly turned their bows south, and the men got their last look at England as St. Catherine's Point, on the southeast tip of the Isle of Wight, merged into the misty horizon. Nothing now but ships till the next day. And no one knew what that held for himself or everyone.

Darkness, and exactly as planned, the forces moving east from Devon and the West generally veered to starboard. Every ship and craft seemed to be on the move at last. And apart from the thousands of landing craft themselves, Neptune needed 8 battle-ships, and monitors, 22 cruisers, 93 destroyers, 450 escorts and minesweepers and 360 M.L.s, M.T.B.s and kindred craft.

Past were the days of camouflage and concealment. Pluto and Bombardon had been hidden successfully; landing craft had emerged from their rivers and creeks; and the first sections of the floating breakwater were on their way from Portland, round to the south of the Island to Area Z. The Green Howards sailed out of the Solent in a high wind, but the evening kept clear. So clear that they saw people and cars moving in a different world on the Isle of Wight.

One of the earliest casualties—soon recovered—was L.C.A. 712. The rising seas battered her badly and she had difficulty in slipping her tow. Lieutenant R. Murray, R.N.V.R., persevered, however, and she took her place in the line southward. Another L.C.A. shipped a lot of water as soon as she started south, yet despite this and a broken tow rope, she met her deadline off Normandy—

with assault troops soaked to the skin. The weather was keeping to Stagg's promise of rough on Monday and better on Tuesday for D-Day. Force U—the unlucky Americans affected by the post-ponement—still met stormy seas and their commanding officers battled on through them all, spending a total of 70 hours on their bridges continuously. Nearly three days and nights without sleep. Out of the 128 tank-landing craft in Group U2A of this famous force, only seven failed to take part in the assault, due to engine troubles as well as the weather. A phenomenal percentage of 95.

But still all was anticlimax. The quiet before the storm. As dusk fell, a reconnaissance aircraft saw the parallel wakes of craft as they plodded and plied on. On into the night.

Long before day dawned, the realization slowly came to Admiral Ramsay that complete tactical surprise was being achieved. And because of it, the whole operation began to take on unreality. Was it really possible that three thousand landing craft and all their attendant ships could cross the Channel without the normally efficient Germans knowing—either by agents or observation?

The sullen oily sea of the gray day turned into a black mass of surging liquid. But by 0200, Force U, nearly a thousand ships strong, was maneuvering undetected off the Contenin peninsula only twelve miles northeast of the Utah landing beaches. Overhead they heard the familiar friendly drone of aircraft carrying airborne troops to precise points on the peninsula. Gradually the 30,000 men and 3,500 vehicles approached the shore. Still there was no sign of awareness. Even the E-boats due to patrol the Seine Bay had turned back to Cherbourg because of the bad weather. The radar jamming of enemy stations was succeeding, for even as they got nearer inshore, the coastal batteries were still silent. Perhaps they had been hit by the hail of bombs from Lancasters which drenched batteries all along the coast during the night without revealing the invasion area.

Also twelve miles offshore, in channels 3 and 4, Force O halted at 0300 to lower their landing craft from the parent vessels which had borne them across so far. The sea swirled below the craft until they hit with a jolt and a shower of spray. Many of the men were sick long before the assault. The sea swamped some of the craft almost as soon as they were on their own, and several sank. Men drowned, dragged down by the weight of the gear and the rough rollers. Others were hauled to safety. Luckier landing craft shipped gallons of water and only baling by tin hats saved them from a fate similar to the ones swamped. One battle against sinking, the next to beat seasickness, and soon the Germans to be faced.

Casualties were light in the assault craft, but the special DD tanks met a host of tragedies. Because of the sea, one battalion of tank-landing craft could not launch these amphibious vehicles. The other battalion risked twenty-nine, but a number of these at once sank to the bottom four miles out to sea; others were swamped during the long run-in; and of all twenty-nine, only two were to reach the shore. Men struggled to get free from their amphibious coffins, choked with water, died.

Even the troops in ordinary landing craft were chilled, cramped and weakened by seasickness: the worst way possible to await an assault which was to many of them a baptism of fire. Shivering, they lived through the ordeal in advance many times that night.

Because of the danger of enemy shore batteries, the "lowering positions" from the mother ships had been fixed for the Western Task Force at 10 to 11¼ miles from the shore, so that they would be beyond range if discovered by the defenses by the time of transferring forces to the landing craft. The distance also put them outside the area known to be mined. This long haul to shore, coupled to the relentlessly rough sea rolling around them, contributed to the tragic losses sustained by the Americans.

Proceeding in parallel along channels 5 to 10, Forces S and J stole still farther inshore before reaching their agreed lowering positions. Seven to eight miles out, they prepared for the final assault. Over to the left, Le Havre still slumbered. The waves were four feet now, and the 15 m.p.h. wind helped to drown any sounds of the approaching invaders. Clouds thickened through the night. Now they were within range of the heavy guns of Le Havre. Force S, the 3rd British Division with all its supporting units, anchored uneasily at this assembly point, not knowing for sure if the German radar were working or not. In fact, it was not—nor one of the batteries—due to a recent raid by Bomber Command.

The first, false dawn etched a mast and funnel in the sky. Then as faint light fell over the fleet, a squadron of aircraft flew low over the area laying an enveloping smoke screen to the east. The black fog blanketed the whole force from the Le Havre coast just at the critical moment before bombardment.

Dawn now—and the first fighting. Three E-boats and some armed trawlers headed out of Havre about 0515, just as Bombarding Force D arrived in position on the eastern flank. They were spotted indistinctly against the land and the order at once went to Allied aircraft overhead:

"Make smoke."

The aircraft flew in low over the sea and laid their smoke screen in seconds, but from behind it the Germans fired a group of torpedoes. The escorting warships *Warspite* and *Ramillies* were able to track these, although two tore right between the warships, uncomfortably close. Suddenly there came an unmistakable sound: the shattering crack of sudden explosion. And in the dull dawn, flames were licking and lashing the deck of the Norwegian destroyer *Svenner*. The Allies opened fire and soon sank one of the trawlers and damaged another. The attack was not renewed, and this hit-and-run raid was the German navy's total effort on D-Day. Fire gripped the destroyer now, as she slipped lower in the water. The blaze became a belch of black, acrid smoke. And slowly she sank.

The assault was soon to start, and back aboard the midget subs the vital hour neared. X.20 marked the spot for Force J, as the coast outline of Juno beach was indistinct. And X.23 stood guard on the surface off the Orne so that Force S should not go too far east.

There was not a sound or sign on the air till Honour heard the first faint throbbing through the water. It came, a dull, droning soulless sound, but with the recognizably regular beat of engines. Ships' motors bringing the armada in right on time. Then heaving low over the horizon, they advanced. L.C.A.s, L.C.I.s, L.C.T.s; L.C.F.s, L.C.S.s, L.C.G.s. Landing ships and headquarters ships. DUKWs and "Rhino" craft. Twenty, thirty, forty ships in a column, the lines reaching right away to port and starboard. But mainly on the port side as the X-craft was more or less the limit of the eastern assault line. Closer, closer, till after all the solitude of the submarine over the last three days, this seemed like a miracle. Men crouched low just above the outline of their landing craft. A host of heads bent on a purpose as proud as any in history.

Hundreds of men—like Corporal George Tandy, Royal Marines, coxwain of L.C.A. 786, aged nineteen. Seven miles out in the still-swirling sea, his assault landing craft lost its steering wheel while being lowered from the parent ship. The crew's duty was to get the thirty-two soldiers in that craft ashore, and in such a sea only one way existed to do it. Tandy slipped over the stern and stood with one foot on the rudder guard and guided the rudder with the other. With fearful frequency the sea hoisted him high in the air and then plunged him back into its pounding waters. For four and a half long hours Tandy stuck it, through mines and everything else. Numbed, bruised, bewildered; but alive.

As L.C.A. 786 and all the others crept closer to the coast, the battleships braced themselves for the attack. Slowly the angles of their guns widened to the exact elevation. Thin fingers poised, pointing to land—and the day of reckoning. D-Day.

Half a dozen deep beside the jetty of an English port, camouflaged landing craft await the men and materials which they will transport to Normandy.

Symbolising the entire Operation Overlord, is this landing craft in the chilly dawn waters. Soon they will be ashore, but after that—no-one knows.

Paratroops smear their faces with black grease while waiting to embark. They were the spearhead of the whole invasion, dropping as they did several hours ahead of the main sea force landing.

Almost airborne. The famous British paratroops line up on the evening of D-1 to embark. With the American air troops, they were the first Allies on enemy soil—soon after midnight.

Morning of D-Day. Aircraft towing gliders with troops to reinforce the early airborne landings. They met anti-aircraft fire but no enemy fighter planes.

Their duty done, these Horsa gliders make a fantastic pattern amid the fields near Caen. The fuselages are all detached on landing for quick unloading.

The Armada advances. An inspiring sight as thousands of ships and craft in line astern plough south to France.

Laden with 90 lb. of kit and ammunition boxes each, they struggle through water up to their chests, trying to keep the powder dry.

British amphibious tanks make landfall—and one is at once set on fire. Others plod up the beaches through morning mist and a maze of deathly obstacles.

Ramps ready. Infantry keep low as their craft comes in. The British amphibious tanks are already ashore, helping to cover the assault, but it is still dangerous down those ramps.

American troops plunge into the surf to wade ashore to the Normandy beach to support other troops fighting on the northern coast of France.

The French commandos are in a hurry. They have come complete with bicycles. There's a reason for this. They must get off this particular beach as quickly as possible.

Blazing bedlam, as British troops shelter behind tanks from shells and mortar fire. Until the barrage ends, and the mines are cleared, the tanks cannot advance inland.

Tanks and other mobile units advance inland against heavy fire. Here a shell explodes right in front of one.

The Normandy shore soon after D-Day—ships dotting the waters, material crowding the beach and U.S. soldiers plodding inland to reinforce the firing line.

The Yanks in the Eto: "After we got a toehold, the stuff just poured in. Some guy in my outfit said he was coming back to take a swim some day."

Eleven

THE CHANNEL STOPPED YOU, BUT NOT US was chalked in foot-high letters on an airborne glider during the evening of D—1. The blackened faces of paratroopers contrasted with the white chalk. And they did not seem to mind that the glider was numbered 13. Camouflage sprouted through the netting over their tin helmets. In smaller letters beside the main message, one of them wrote carefully: *Remember Coventry, Plymouth, Bristol, London. Now it's our turn.*

Over at another airfield preparing for flight on D-Day, troops sweated and heaved as they shoved a jeep up a ramp into a glider. Anti-aircraft guns were also loaded, together with a mass of equipment needed to ward off German counterattacks.

Earlier, Eisenhower had talked to American airborne forces as they quit their canvas tents to get ready for the flight. And Air Chief Marshal Leigh-Mallory had gone round to every airfield from which Allied airborne forces would be taking off later that night of June 5.

At 2230 that night, sixty men of the 22nd Independent Parachute Company were drinking tea out of mugs from a mobile canteen and smoking beside half a dozen Albemarle aircraft on the runway of Harwell. These men were to be the pathfinders for the 6th Airborne Division. Not only black, but brown and green paint darkened their faces, and among as much as 100 pounds of gear they carried Sten guns, ammunition, knives and grenades, plus a bag of radar beacons and lights strapped to one leg of each man for marking the dropping zones.

Another twenty minutes and the paratroops filed into their planes. Darkness now, as at 2303 the first Albemarle taxied down

97

the runway, cleared the hedges at the perimeter, and droned south. The other five followed rapidly. Seventy-seven minutes later, at 0020 on D-Day, they were over the three dropping zones. The moon shone in a clear sky, but despite this advantage, and the fact that half the aircraft ran in twice or more, only one "stick" of paratroops landed correctly on the three zones. All the visual beacons for one zone were lost or damaged in the drop.

The pathfinders parachuting down near Ranville were scattered principally by the high wind which carried them east of the intended zone. Since the main force they were to guide would be due in under half an hour they had no time to try and recover. Instead they lit their beacons there.

Due to drop at the same time as the pathfinders was a *coup de main* force under the command of Major R. J. Howard. Their tasks were to capture intact two vital bridges: the one on the only through road over the River Orne, the other over the canal between Caen and the sea.

Theirs was an airborne assault by gliders—like the later main force—towed by Halifax bombers. At exactly 0015, the bombers slipped their tows and went on to attack Caen, while the gliders circled silently down. Their audacious assault plan was to crash-land on their actual objectives. Howard was in the leading glider headed for the canal bridge, and its wheels gripped into the ground only 47 yards (who measured that?) from the eastern end of the bridge. It grasshoppered the rest of the way, ending in barbed wire with its nose broken. Howard and his men had to grope their way out via the cockpit instead of the door. The two other gliders aimed at the canal bridge crash-landed close behind them. The enemy was sheltering from the Halifaxes' sudden attack on Caen, so Howard's men raced on to take the bridge. A spatter of machine-gun fire from the far side killed the commander of the first platoon. They cleared a pillbox and nearby network of trenches, and ensured that the bridge would not be blown up by the enemy.

Eight hundred yards to the east, about the same time, the other gliders landed less accurately. But two of the three platoons got to their bridge over the Orne within minutes to find it undefended. Consolidating the captures, they found that although the Germans had prepared both bridges for blowing, no alarm had reached them so the charges were not in position.

The bridgeheads had been taken. They must be held until the main forces reinforced and relieved them.

Half an hour after the pathfinder drops, and just about the moment the two bridges fell, the 5th Parachute Brigade joined the invasion. Their story started at 2000 hours on the evening of June 5 when the 7th Battalion was roused from a final sleep before battle. All identification by letters or other evidence was surrendered, and 620 men went out to the airfield in thirty-three lorries, one for each Stirling plane that would carry them. There was no wisecracking now, only an occasional quiet song and the usual routine of sipping mugs of tea, and smearing dark camouflage on their faces so no sniper could distinguish them in the black of night. Collapsible dinghies were even crammed into some of their kit bags, since they would be operating near two rivers and might need to cross one or the other.

The briefing over, they synchronized watches as they stood before propellers waiting to turn. Then they stepped off English earth and soon the Stirlings climbed into the sky of this immortal night and flew high over the Channel.

At a quarter to one, low cloud blew over the drop zone, obscuring some of the beacons and making accurate navigation impossible. The Stirlings circled trying to find the exact spot. Suddenly, anti-aircraft, alerted by the pathfinders, spat shells and tracer upward, and flak hit two of the thirty-three Stirlings. The night wind fanned the fire and a deadly drone presaged the start of a spiral down, down into the French fields they sought to liberate. Two Stirlings, forty paratroops and the crews.

Promptly at 0050, the other 31 aircraft came in low over the zone and dropped their human loads. The descent took only about ten seconds, but to the paratroopers exposed to the German fire from below it seemed an eternity.

Lieutenant Colonel Pine-Coffin was in command of this battalion drop, which due to the pathfinders' problems and the low cloud, landed badly scattered. Thus although they came down quite near the drop zone many of the men were unable to find it.

99

Luckily Pine-Coffin managed to get his bearings when a flare from one of the aircraft silhouetted the old church at Ranville, which had stood serenely for six centuries.

Pine-Coffin found Lieutenant Rogers and together they slowly assembled some men with the aid of Rogers' Aldis lamp which blinked out as a prearranged signal to the troops. For Rogers himself, however, his signal might well have been fatal if it had attracted enemy fire toward him, but in the confusion he had little time to dwell on this.

The invaders were not exactly keeping their arrival secret for as another means of attracting the men to their commander a private sounded their regimental call on a bugle! By 0215 this combination of blinking and bugling mustered about 250 of the 620 men dropped from the thirty-one aircraft. They dared not delay any longer, as firing from the canal bridge suggested that they were already needed there. When they reached the bridge, however, they found that the firing had been no more than ammunition exploding in a German tank; and soon Major R. J. Howard's radio code signals of "Ham and Jam" told them that both bridges were safely in British hands. With real relief they ditched their dinghies and by 0300 were in their planned positions near the bridges. Many of the men, however, were without their special weapons which had been lost somewhere in the French fields as a result of the unlucky air drop.

Two hundred and fifty men with a few pistols and Sten guns, but no 3-inch mortars or medium machine guns. It is no wonder Pine-Coffin was not too confident of their ability to hold the bridges. But before long, A Company had settled into the village of Benouville, B Company in the hamlet of Le Port with one platoon actually on the bridge over the Orne. In addition Pine-Coffin had C Company in reserve.

"The hour before dawn" to A Company will always mean the moment at Benouville when the Germans suddenly attacked them on three sides simultaneously. The sounds of the attack reaching the other companies suggested that the attack was in some strength, so Lieutenant MacDonald led twenty men from the reserve C Company, ill-armed for such a task, in an assault aimed at breaking through to Benouville. This they did, fighting all the way till they found A Company still warding off attacks on all three sides.

Two platoons of B Company, meanwhile, dug into the escarpment of Le Port, while the third platoon deployed around the canal bridge. One platoon to hold a vital canal bridge was scarcely what the planners had intended, and sporadic fire kept the men in constant fear of their lives, and made them wish for the extra paratroops dropped far from the right zone. One of their two particular aircraft discharged its troops no less than twelve miles from the center of the zone. They might just as well have been 1200 miles away at this precise moment.

At 2330 on June 5 the first of the Stirlings that were to carry the 12th Battalion gave a mechanical cough as its engines spluttered to life. The battalion's objective was the village of Le Bas de Ranville, and like the rest of the brigade, they had a quiet flight across the Channel. As the first aircraft approached the coast, one of the air crew removed the hatches and they could dimly see the white waves breaking on the beach, lines similar to the identity stripes painted around the body of their aircraft. Then from sea, beach and cliffs the view changed to strange silhouettes of woods, and the patterns of fields and hedges. A red light blazed, then a green one and the parachutes fluttered out and floated down.

It was not until about 0200 that the 12th Battalion mustered sufficient strength to make a start toward their goal of Le Bas de Ranville. Lieutenant Colonel A. P. Johnson, commanding the battalion, collected more men who had landed outside the drop zone as he advanced on the village.

Then came their first brush with the enemy. Just as they were on the village's outskirts they suddenly saw two vehicles bearing down on them.

"Fire!" an officer called out.

A German motorcyclist slid off his machine which careened madly on and into a ditch. The other vehicle, an armored car, burst through however only to be stopped at the approaches to the bridge where a hail of fire sent it lurching off the road. From it staggered the German officer responsible for the defenses of the bridges—belatedly. Investigation of the car revealed the remains of a meal as well as some rouge and face powder. Obviously the armored car's crew had plans other than fighting an engagement with British paratroopers.

Meanwhile the 13th battalion began work on their particular piece of the jigsaw—clearing the adjacent village of Ranville and its vital bridges over the Orne. Vital, too, was the task of removing the sharply pointed anti-airborne poles which dotted the ground earmarked for glider landings later in this eventful night.

Those of the 13th who came to earth in the specified area fared well, but many of the rest—nearly half of the battalion's strength—came to grief amid the surrounding trees. Desperately they tried to free themselves in the gloom of the woodlands, but a number were found and shot by the Germans. But the majority of the battalion were able to respond to the brigade's hunting horns which blared out into the night as if attached to some phantom pack. By 0230 the enemy garrison in Ranville had been overrun and Ranville fell: the first French village to be liberated.

While this historic if small action went on, the company detailed to clear the landing fields for the gliders was going about its job thoroughly. And back in England the main glider force of 72 machines, with guns, transport, and equipment, prepared to take off. Their time of landing had been worked out for 0330, to allow the force two hours before daybreak in which to complete their missions.

Shortly before 0200 the air armada began to move. The tow planes roared down the runway, their engines racing to take the strain of hauling a glider. Then the tow went taut, the rope quivering into a straight line. Plane and glider gradually moved. The ground slid beneath them; the wheels left it; there was no turning back.

All the paratroops could see as they crouched in their gliders was rain, and now and again a glimpse of light from their particular towing aircraft. Unseen below them the sea armada sailed on south, some ten miles, others fifty miles, from the D-Day coast. Then as the cloud cleared they caught momentary sight of the slow-moving ships. Then back in the cloud again, the gliders' wings wobbling in the gusty gale.

Nought three hundred, and the enemy coast below. Denser cloud now, and no sign of even the tow plane's rear light. Just when they really needed good visibility, the clouds closed in on them. Then the inevitable flak began; a kaleidoscope of color flashing all about them. Seventy-two gliders and as many tow planes seemed silhouetted at once, as if they were frozen still in the sky. Sitting targets at 2500 feet. One glider was hit just enough to throw it off balance, which was dangerous since neither the towing aircraft nor the gliders themselves could maneuver much while they were still linked. Over on one side, another glider took a direct hit, and twenty-six men plus the pilot perished. Then another glider went down.

Over the Channel the men had sung gaily. Not now.

Below they saw the weaving, watery lines of the Orne and the Canal de Caen threading through the land. They were over the target area now, but *they* were the targets. Below, the beacons and the flak intermingled in one colorful confusion.

Then one by one the tows parted. The gliders wavered in the wind, then slowly their noses angled down through the flak. One last magic moment of quiet after they were below the flak and before they scraped the ground. A last dive in the dark, with beacons, lights, roads, barns, and other unidentifiable shapes lurching past on each side of them. Any second now. This was exactly how the first assault troops would be feeling a few hours later on the beaches. But for the paratroops the moment of truth had come sooner.

Obstacle posts were torn or ripped right out of the ground as the splitting and splintering gliders screeched to a halt, some upright, others overturned, others actually on end with their tails pointing high to heaven. The men clambered into the grain field which was their airfield, leaving a litter of gliders facing in every direction of the compass, crazily up against hedges or actually touching one another. But however the airborne men had arrived, they were here, that was the important thing: in the right place at the right time.

While German guns still fired into a sky so lately filled with the slow, vulnerable gliders, the men moved quickly through the ripening grain. And then came the sounds of equipment being moved into action stations. On the perimeter of the field a sentry barked a challenge, and the code name response came at once.

To an observer, the field presented an alarming panorama. The whole zone seemed to be full of wrecked gliders. And even as the early arrivals glanced at the apparent desolation, a latecomer swung in low over the field and smashed straight into a house at its perimeter. In all, however, two out of every three gliders landed safely and accurately. Thus most of the men and their weapons came in safely, while ten of the eighteen antitank guns landed in working order.

Now as quickly as they could they moved off toward Ranville church, the only opposition they sighted being a rapidly retreating German military car. Soon afterwards the British held their first prisoner—a chestnut-brown horse which had been minding its own business on the landing zone! The animal came under the care of Brigadier Richard Gale's aide-de-camp and was brought to the battalion's temporary headquarters at Ranville. Gale himself, ignoring the occasional snipers' bullets, went off in a jeep to survey the situation at the bridges the British held.

The airborne operation as a whole proved to be far from plain sailing, or flying. One Albemarle tried seven times to find the drop zone, but before it could do so it was hit by flak and had to turn and head for home. At the actual moment the shell exploded the 3rd Parachute Brigade Major—W. A. C. Collingwood—was waiting to jump. The blast blew him through the plane's opening and his line wound round one of his legs. As the aircraft headed sadly north once more, he hung beneath it for half an hour, with a 60-pound kit bag weighting his other leg. Eventually the men inside the plane succeeded in hoisting him aboard the Albemarle again. The postscript was that the plane got back to England and Collingwood insisted on joining his brigade, which he did later on D-Day.

The brigade's mission was a far-flung operation, one not made easier by the bad night which inevitably caused an inaccurate drop.

Its task was to destroy the bridges in the Dives Valley and seize a ridge between the Dives and the Orne. In fact, the two rivers proved indistinguishable from the air, a fact which constituted an unexpected hurdle. Coming into this chaos, the aircraft encountered ack-ack fire which forced them to undertake urgent evasive action, with the result that Brigadier S. J. L. Hill and his men jumped while the planes were traveling too fast, and consequently were carried well beyond their goal.

The 1st Canadian Parachute Battalion dropped between 0100 and 0130 over an area forty times as large as planned. And one aircraft was forced to return home to Down Ampney without dropping any of its troops when, as it took a hit from enemy flak in its fuselage, a parachutist fell into—instead of through—the exit and wedged it tight shut until the plane was minutes and miles past the right area!

As another aircraft crossed the mouth of the Canal de Caen it was met by a stream of tracer which shrieked past only 15 feet to starboard. The plane at once swung violently left, and when the men had sorted themselves out they found that they had altered course so severely that following pilots probably confused the Orne and Dives rivers. Many of the eighty-six Canadians taken prisoner by the Germans as a result of the scattered drop rejoined their units soon afterwards—testimony to their ingenuity under any circumstances, foreseen or otherwise.

Several sticks of the 9th and 1st Canadian Parachute Battalions actually dropped into the River Dives or in the flooded, desolate wastelands beside it. Some men were drowned in these swamps; just one tragic way of dying on this day of days.

Another group, under Lieutenant Colonel Alastair Pearson, dropped in a much more scattered pattern than had ever been intended, and some of the men as a result were trapped in the tree-tops of the Bois de Bavent. Pearson dropped safely, but he had scarcely shaken himself free of his harness when a bullet hit him in the hand. Despite the fact that he was losing blood steadily, he went on with his duty and rounded up enough men to set about the group's job of destroying the bridges.

Four of the five bridges over the Dives were blown up as rehearsed, but the fifth only succumbed as a result of a daring impro-visation. Pearson's men met a group of Royal Engineers who had landed north of the Bois de Bavent to whom they explained that they had not enough explosive left for the last bridge. So the sappers piled the necessary charges into a jeep, drove straight through the German-held town of Troarn, miraculously surviving machine-gun fire from point-blank range, and managed to blow a gaping gap in the last bridge.

Like so many other airborne units, the 1st Canadian Battalion made a badly scattered drop and had some of its men cut off from the rest by woods or marshes, and taken prisoner. The Germans lined up five of these Canadians and summarily shot them. Four died, but the fifth was only wounded in the leg and somehow slipped away, somehow made contact with the Resistance, and was soon hobbling off to rejoin his unit. Needless to say, the Canadians succeeded in blowing their bridges over the Dives and at Robehomme.

Captain R. M. E. Kerr of the British 13th Battalion actually landed right in the River Dives, but managed to struggle free from his harness, stagger ashore, soaked and shivering, and find a farm where four other parachutists had also taken shelter. The French family greeted them warmly, even though it was in the middle of the night, and a young boy offered to guide them to their objective of Varaville.

With his help they found the place at about 0330, but violent enemy activity forbade their entering it, and they instead skirted the village and entered a wood. Quite suddenly a German patrol appeared from nowhere and in the resultant melee a grenade burst right over the boy's head. This was war now.

Now on to the main mission of the 3rd Parachute Brigade: to destroy the dangerous enemy battery on the coast near Merville.

Brigadier Gale said: "The Hun thinks that only a bloody fool will go there. That's why we're going!"

To Lieutenant-Colonel T. B. H. Otway, Royal Ulster Rifles, and the 9th Battalion fell the duty of destroying the battery: a strong-point with four 150-mm. guns, housed in thick concrete, and protected by ten machine guns, mines, and other elaborate defenses. Otway had to silence the battery by half an hour before first light, so that the invasion fleet could begin the approach knowing the beaches west of the Orne estuary would be safe from the fire from Merville, which could conceivably knock out enough of the British invasion forces to endanger the entire operation. The German garrison was thought to number about 180 men.

An involved plan had been worked out which included eleven separate parties, each with a specific job to do. In addition, three troop-carrying gliders were to crash their way right into the midst of the battery just as the paratroops were due to start their assault.

The glider force and two other parties took off from Brize Norton and Harwell in England about half past eleven, the rest earlier at 2310. The reconnaissance party was the first to drop so it could mark the drop zone and find a route through the defenses to the battery. Wearing jump suits decorated with an alarming skull and crossbones marked in luminous paint on the left breast, they dropped quite close to their intended spot.

Then the next part of the plan, scheduled for 0030 and 0040, went into operation as a hundred Lancaster bombers flew in over the battery in an attack designed to saturate it before the start of the main airborne assault. Unfortunately the weather was again against the Allies, and not at all good for high-level night bombing. A number of great 4,000-pound bombs screamed down through the clouds and exploded uselessly half a mile from their target. In fact one or two of them actually fell near the airborne reconnaissance group as it groped its way toward the battery.

Now came the main drop which fell four minutes away from the zone as, already confusing the mouths of the Orne and Dives in the darkness, the pilots also had to contend with heavy flak. Veering violently to evade it, they gave the paratroops a nasty few minutes. Men with 80-pound loads plus parachutes were flung all over the aircraft as they swerved to escape the probing searchlights. But there was nothing for it but to go ahead with the drop—despite the conditions. The lines of paratroops groped their way out of lurching aircraft in a manner as far from their disciplined descents as is possible to imagine.

Thus instead of a drop concentrated into an area roughly a mile long by half a mile wide, the paratroops were spread over an area of roughly some 50 square miles about the Merville battery. The stick earning the doubtful distinction of landing farthest from the target came down a full thirty miles away! So much for the weeks of rigorous rehearsal.

This was bad enough, but worse followed as five equipment gliders were lost. A strong squall over the Channel strained and finally snapped their tow ropes, and the quintet glided helplessly down into the sea, taking their antitank guns, jeeps and other equipment with them. So equipment Otway and his men would need before many more minutes had elapsed was irretrievably lost.

Meanwhile Otway himself was flung from his Dakota as it was banking steeply to escape ground fire. Then of all places to land, he and two other men drifted down into a garden beside the H. Q. of a German unit, some distance from Merville. The Germans at once fired on them but luckily their aim was poor and none of the trio was hit. Then Otway's batman clambered onto the roof of the greenhouse attached to the house and heaved a brick through a window. The Germans naturally assumed this must be a grenade and in the resultant confusion the trio of British paratroops escaped.

As rapidly as they could they made their way toward the rendezvous, but when they reached it, they found that practically nothing had gone according to plan. All the plans on which they had been so carefully briefed for five full days were at once rendered useless when Otway realized at 0250 that the total remaining strength of the battalion was only 150 men with twenty lengths of Bangalore torpedo. Gone were the 3-inch mortars; the 6-pounder guns; the jeeps; the trailers; the glider stores; the sappers; the field ambulance; the mine detectors. On the credit side they had some signal flares, a machine gun, half of one sniping party, and six medical orderlies who would be needed before much longer. In one way this simplified the situation. Yet looked at soberly, it seemed insane to go on.

Otway decided to advance at once, and waste no more time looking for guns which might have dropped almost anywhere in Normandy. For they were still a mile and a half from Merville. So they set out—decimated but determined.

One part of the plan which came off more or less as anticipated was their meeting with Major G. Smith and the reconnaissance party, who were already in the environs of the battery. Smith told Otway that he and his men had cut one fence, traversed a mine field inside it, and spent a half hour attempting to place the exact locations of the sentry posts from the sounds of the Germans on guard. In fact one German patrol had passed no more than two feet from where they lay.

Otway and the main force now advanced to the party actually charged with penetrating the mine field. Despite trip wires and other obstacles which were all doubly dangerous in the dark, these men had found a route through the mines and marked it without a single casualty. The way was thus clear to the inner wire.

0424: only a few minutes to zero hour, and now two of the three gliders bearing the special, almost suicidal, assault teams arrived overhead as scheduled. Alas, the tow rope of the third had parted far too soon, and the glider had to land in England.

But now two had arrived. Both tugs and gliders took hit after hit from tracers from the ground which tore upwards toward them. But despite this inferno, one of the planes circled the battery four times before releasing its glider. But since the paratroops could not fire the planned star shells, they had been lost in the drop—the pilot of one glider understandably became confused and mistook the village of Merville for the battery. At the last moment he realized his mistake and swung the glider clear of the village, but it still came down some four miles away.

So then there was one. Anti-aircraft fire had already hit four of the special troops in the last glider, and with the machine itself starting to smolder, the pilot decided he must get down without delay. Spotting a large field a short distance from the battery, he headed for it, only suddenly to see a MINEN sign. The wheels of the glider were on the grass, yet somehow he managed to hoist it clear of the ground, over a hedge and road, and bring it down again in a safer spot. The glider was wingless and burning now, and as the men —the wounded as well as the fit—plunged from it they took on the Germans in a useful diversionary action which helped to leave Otway free for the main assault.

As the glider came to its halt, six enemy machine guns opened fire on Otway's base from *outside* the perimeter. Then four more inside it joined in, bringing the total to ten. Yet somehow with their lone Vickers gun, the assault force silenced three of the German guns, while a diversion group did equally well over on the right flank.

Now the die was cast. About 0435 Otway ordered that the starting signal be given—and the first of the twenty lengths of wire-blowing torpedo shot forward over the uneven ground. These Bangalores did their job well, leaving vital gaps in the wire defenses.

Working their way through mines and the jagged holes caused by exploding shells and bombs, the two assault teams dashed forward in the face of withering machine-gun fire. The plan was far simpler now than originally. One group went for the gunners themselves and closed in mortal combat with them until the sight of the parachutists' skull symbol caused a German to cry out in terror, whereupon his particular group gave in.

The other assault team raced straight for the big guns, fighting their way across the bomb-scarred ground until they saw two of the doors open to the main emplacements. Fingers clamped on triggers, the group fired everything they had through those doors—and the Germans inside quickly surrendered in a panic of self-preservation.

Within minutes the paratroops destroyed three of the big German guns with Gammon bombs and put a fourth out of action by the simple expedient of firing two of its own shells through the barrel simultaneously. The lieutenant whose job it was to check that the guns had definitely been neutralized was fatally hit during the action, but somehow he struggled forward and managed to check that all guns were out of action before he collapsed and died.

Only twelve minutes or so after Otway had given his signal to start the final offensive he was ordering a second signal, this time to the naval force assembled offshore to tell them that the Merville mission was accomplished. For hours the signal officer had carried a companion in the blouse of his battle dress. Now he tenderly drew it out, and a slightly startled pigeon blinked at the scene all around. With a message confirming their victory strapped to its leg, the bird was flung high into the smoky air above the battery, and later on D-Day it landed safe and sound at its destination in England!

Now Otway took stock to find that of his tiny force of 150 men, nearly a half were casualties. Eighty still stood on their feet, the rest were killed, wounded, or missing. So a handful of men with one machine gun had stormed one of the most strongly fortified strongpoints on the French coast, and captured and destroyed it within fifteen minutes of launching the assault.

Half an hour after it was over, H.M.S. *Arethusa* was due to begin the bombardment—starting signal for the invasion by sea.

But the stage was not yet set from both wings for the final, withering onslaught. While the British paratroops stormed Merville and the bridges around the vital Caen area to the east, away on the west the Americans aimed to do the same thing at Sainte Mère Eglise behind the Utah beach.

In the fiery afterglow of a storm-streaked sunset, Eisenhower hurried around seven southern airfields to talk to his paratroops; their helmets dotted with camouflage, faces daubed dark. Before he was back at Southwick, the aircraft were airborne.

Specifically, their tasks were for the 101st Airborne Division to ensure the exits from the Utah beach by occupying the causeways inland over the swampy ground. Another regiment had to follow the same pattern as over the Orne and blow up the bridges along the Douve. The 82nd Division dropping near Sainte Mère Eglise were to see that the seaborne forces would not be hemmed in behind a series of inland inundations.

So much for the theory.

Ahead of the waves of carriers, fighters created cover and a clear route for the first paratroops—the pathfinders. These twenty pathfinder aircraft preceded the main force of 432 carriers bearing 6,600 paratroops of the 101st Division. The main force took off at 2215. Despite having to fly in low and vulnerable to flak, these first planes reached the six dropping zones, for both divisions, partly through the aid of a thick, enveloping cloudbank. But these same clouds made accuracy very difficult for the following air-craft. Formations flew tight until they reached the French coast, but then the flak flew into them. One plane lurched to a hit, its port engines afire. Wheeling round desperately to head for home, it left a sheet of fire; a searing semicircle in the sky as it spiraled downward. Then the seconds passed until a sudden mushroom of flame leaped up from the ground.

Other aircraft veered violently to escape the flak, so that they were flying too fast and high for accurate jumps. But the men piled out, black shapes slipping from the belly of the planes. Operation Albany was on. Actually the flak fire did comparatively little damage due to the cloud conditions, but the human element, so often overlooked, produced an effect not envisaged. For most of the planes' pilots this was their battle baptism, and the anti-aircraft fire unleashed against them caused excessive evasive action.

The 101st Division thus dropped from aircraft desperately trying to shake off the shattering shock of flak-bursts. Thus the men were strewn over a length of landscape of 25 miles. They were literally pitchforked from wildly weaving aircraft without any idea where they would come down. As the sound of shells and engines throbbed away above, the scattered parachutes billowed out unseen, their gray-green khaki colorings invisible in the 0130 darkness of D-Day just begun.

Some of the Americans fell even farther afield, miles from their objectives during the middle of the night in a foreign land where one field seemed indistinguishable from the next. Someone, however, had thought of this, and the whole division carried clicking snappers which they sounded to try and find each other.

Typical of the confusion was the case of Lieutenant Colonel Robert Cole, who actually landed near Sainte Mère Eglise, where he collected thirty men of his own division and a few from the 82nd Division. Backtracking north, they headed for the two northern exits of the beach and the group snowballed to seventy-five men. On the way they met and killed some of an enemy convoy, then moved on toward the coast.

The battalions aiming to capture the southern beach exits also had bad drops; in one instance, 81 planes were scheduled to drop their troops in Zone C, and actually only ten aircraft found their mark.

The Germans had evidently anticipated a drop in Zone D, for

the aircraft ran into concentrated ack-ack fire. An oil-soaked building near the drop field was set on fire as they actually floated down toward it, followed by the familiar deadly chatter of machine guns and *clonk* of mortars. Silhouetted with all their chutes and supports, a number of the Americans were riddled in the air before they had a chance to reply.

It was too soon yet to count the cost, but in fact only about a thousand of the 6,600 men in the division reached their rendezvous by dawn. And far more serious, some fifteen hundred were killed or captured, while more than half of their equipment dropped was lost as the bundles fell futilely into the surrounding swamps or into fields covered by enemy fire.

They needed that lost equipment and ammunition desperately. Captain Charles Shettle came down near Angoville-au-Plain and actually walked toward the town looking for his men. He found fourteen men and by the time he had reached the northern bridge at Le Port about 0430, the group had risen to thirty-three men. Despite fire from the opposite bank, they forced a crossing and occupied the east side. This scratch bridgehead force accounted for a few of the enemy and their machine guns, but by dawn the fight became unequal as the Americans ran low on ammunition—lying in the swamps—and with no hope of friendly forces to reinforce them. They withdrew to the west bank soon afterward and held it.

Another objective of the American 101st Division was the lock on the Douve at La Barquette. Again the inaccurate drop nearly caused complete failure of this mission right at the outset. Some of the sticks of paratroops bumped down deep in enemy territory; others in swampy bottom lands to the west. One command's personnel was particularly hard hit: the commanding officer was killed almost at once and his executive officer captured. All the other company commanders and staff were missing initially.

In light of this, an accident which partly saved the day could be called doubly providential. As the jump signal flashed in Colonel Johnson's plane, a bundle of equipment became tightly wedged in the drop door! There were a furious few seconds while they fought to free it. Then it sailed out. But if Johnson and his men had jumped on the signal, they would have found that they had unloaded prematurely and were short of their zone.

Moving south, Johnson collected 150 miscellaneous men and advanced to a junction north of the lock. A force of fifty men reached the lock in a single dramatic dash, and dug in on the soft ground before the enemy could bring it under shellfire.

Then just in time, 51 gliders soared out of the early sky to reinforce the 101st Division. The bodies of the great gliders churned up the French earth as they scraped in to land accurately beside the main rendezvous. Welcome white-painted stars near their tails cheered the scattered Americans, who saw them from their various vantage points.

These 51 Waco gliders, carrying command personnel and anti-tank weapons, as well as 150 troops, landed just before dawn. This type of landing had never been attempted before without full daylight, and although they came in accurately, many of them were wrecked as they hit the small Normandy fields. Men and materials both suffered, and Brigadier General Don Pratt, second in command of the 101st, was killed in landing. The losses remained reasonable, however, and with the extra troops, Major General Taylor, commanding the 101st, secured all the vital exits from the western causeways leading off the Utah beach, including the villages of Pouppeville and St. Martin-de-Varreville. So although they could not blow the bridges, they had succeeded in their main task.

An hour after the main 101st sticks were dropped, the 82nd Division followed and fell within two or three miles of the drop zone. This was, in the words of the official account, "far from good." Indeed many men found themselves nearer the 101st and actually fought with elements of the other division for days.

In contrast to the other two divisions the one earmarked to take Sainte Mère Église fell almost to a pinpoint. About half the force of 2,200 men landed in the drop zone, and most of the others assembled quite quickly. Fortunate to find themselves in an area almost free of Germans, they took advantage of their luck. They landed at 0230. By 0430, Sainte Mère Eglise was in their hands and the main road from Carentan to Cherbourg successfully cut.

The planes carrying this division ran into fog and flak—as a change from cloud—and the chances of a tight drop seemed slim. But some of the planes, which had moved out to prevent possible collisions, circled back before flashing the green light. The result: the good drop indicated.

Colonel Krause learned from a Frenchman that the Germans had recently established themselves along the roads outside the town, so he planned to take the town and erect road blocks before daylight.

"Go directly into the town without searching buildings," he told them, "and while it's dark use only knives, bayonets and grenades." This was so that German small-arms fire could be spotted by sight and sound.

The paratroops streamed silently down the straight main road running right through the town, at the same time outlining its perimeter with other troops. Across the fields, the churchyard, and the compact orchards they moved, till they entirely surrounded the town. Then they raised the very same American flag which they had flown over Naples when the Italian city was entered, and within two hours of their arrival they had made Sainte Mère Eglise the first town to be taken by the Americans in the invasion.

The success at Sainte Mère Eglise assumed added point as a critical situation developed along the line of the Merderet River, where the well-laid plans of the other two divisions went astray as soon as the sticks started to fall in a pattern very different from that planned.

The divisions flew in on time between 0230 and 0300, only to see that the preceding pathfinders had not been able to mark the drop zones because the enemy were actually among them. Puzzled by the absence of marker lights, many pilots overshot the zones, and whole groups of paratroops splashed down in the watery marshes along the Merderet.

Aerial photos showed only this grassy swampland and not the wide flood areas created by closing the La Barquette lock. The grass growing out of this lakeland had sprouted so thickly that from above it looked like a prairie instead of treacherous water several feet deep. Into this water dozens of heavily laden

115

troops were plunged, and far from being an offensive operation, it was necessary to rescue as many as possible.

Only one man in twenty-five of these two divisions came to earth near his intended zone, and the whole force had to fight for its life almost without worrying about destroying bridges over the Douve or the Merderet. Nevertheless, they did fulfill a role in occupying the 91st German Infantry Division, a reserve earmarked to tackle any invasion army on the beaches.

With enemy fire building up in one particular place, countermeasures were held up while the Americans tried to retrieve a jeep and an antitank gun from the marshes where they had fallen.

Men of another battalion under Colonel Timmes established a hold bridgehead at one place, but within an hour it was lost. The German artillery countered quickly. Small-arms fire came from the south and tanks rumbling from the west. So the main force pulled out, leaving the bridgehead in the hands of four officers and eight men. These dozen Americans with grenades, rifles, and one machine gun fought off the enemy—seen now as well as heard—and grenades shattered two of the leading tanks trundling toward the bridge. But they were not equal to armor and had to withdraw.

Dawn brought Operation Detroit and 52 gliders with weapons and transport intended to equip and reinforce the 82nd Division. But once again, accuracy proved the stumbling point and only 22 of them got to the landing zone. Meanwhile, swampland and other hazards had multiplied the difficulties and the engagements of the airborne troops. Instead of two or three neat operations, they fought fifteen to twenty separate little battles, often only a few hundred yards away from each other yet unable to link up or get a clear idea of what was happening or where their services would be needed most. The two American airborne divisions did pave the way for their colleagues landing later, though not as planned; but nothing ever is as planned when war breaks loose on such a scale.

Throughout this night, too, the air was alive in a dozen different ways. Eleven hundred and thirty-six aircraft of Bomber Command thundered through the night to drop 5,853 tons on picked positions such as coast batteries. Again the silent ships heard the reassuring roar of their engines, both before and after the operations, which finished at dawn.

Smaller, secret sorties, too, such as Operation Sunflower, covered the drop of Special Air Service reconnaissance parties in six areas.

Already the enemy's radar stations had been blasted with rockets streaming into unlikely woods, so Leigh-Mallory could report that in the vital period between 0100 and 0400 hours when the assault armada was nearing the lowering positions, only nine enemy radar stations were in operation. And during the whole night, the number of stations active in the Neptune area (the entire invasion coast line) only amounted to 18 out of a normal 92. No station was heard operating at all between Le Havre and Barfleur, the two cape extremities covering the D-Day goal.

No radar warning at all was given of either the sea forces or the airborne operations. While the first paratroops floated down easily, wondering what awaited them, the Luftwaffe's night fighter force was flying furiously around the Amiens area, where electronics had created "ghost squadrons" of Allied bombers requiring interception. Another scientific miracle that further confused the badly bewildered Germans on that night was our dummy parachutists, complete with special delay devices to emit cracking sounds like rifle fire! These were duly reported between Le Havre and Rouen, east of the actual invasion front, after aircraft crews had bundled the dummies out of their planes, chuckling at the thought of the Germans' reactions when they discovered their mistake! Even at 0400, the harassed Von Runstedt could not anticipate the precise places of the main attack. What a business: real paratroops, dummy ones, diversions, tinfoil dropped to simulate ships, and the rest of the ingenious ideas. And all in the middle of the night! Where was the mass attack going to take place? The answer was not long in coming.

Twelve

OUT of the morning mist broke a barrage mightier than sound itself, the concerted crescendo of almost a thousand guns firing in shattering sequence. Across the sea the shells whistled and whined to the Normandy shores, leaving the decks of the ships shuddering with the quivering recoil.

Here was history being made, as cloudy columns of suffocating, smudgy smoke rose in a gray-black blot along the fringe of France. D for Deliverance. Men's hearts hung in their mouths, or their throats—or their stomachs. A glance at a watch; muted mutterings; a prayer; parched tongues.

And above it all the bombardment; an electrifying explosion erupting first from the ships, then flashing across the sullen pre-dawn summer sky and ending ashore. Next the attack by air. Fighter-bombers yelling in at sea level to assault artillery positions inland. And the high-level, aloof drone of one-and-a-third thousand American heavy bombers. Not a single German aircraft took off to interfere. Here, at last, was the reward of the long years of struggling for superiority in the air.

Compressed into thirty mutilating minutes, the U.S. 8th Air Force raid rained down a devastating tonnage of bombs in drops that extended right up to the minute of H-Hour; the time scheduled for the first assault troops to hit each particular beach.

So under an umbrella of pummeling, pounding fire, unequaled in history, the craft crawled in. Dots of hundreds of helmeted heads keeping as low as possible above the sides of the landing craft.

First blood to the Yanks. At H−40 minutes, or 0550, battleships, cruisers and a dozen destroyers of Task Force 125 sent shells streaming into the Utah beach batteries. And as the clock crept round to 0600, 276 Marauder medium bombers laid over 4,000 bombs on seven beach objectives.

Next, while the assault craft came to the last lap before the beaches, the 33 vessels of the Utah beach fire support group joined in to add their quota. Seventeen of these craft mounted rocket launchers and now they discharged their weapons as the first waves of troops were 600 to 700 yards offshore.

Although the coast defenses were not in general as effectively eliminated as had been hoped, the short, shattering bombardments did neutralize them for the vital assault minutes. Entanglements and mine fields were destroyed in some cases, the beach mines exploding adding to the orchestral eruptions all around. The very volume of the fire shook the defenders and paralyzed their communications. Drenched by the double bombardment from sea and air, the defense remained dazed as almost complete surprise appeared to have been achieved.

Even as the telltale wakes of the craft bearing the 4th U.S. Infantry Division neared the shore, the Germans seemed mesmerized by the fantastic ferocity of the onslaught, coming at them from all angles, so that the actual invasion troops met only slight and spasmodic opposition. At Utah, at least, the weather was worse than the fire from the shore.

One of the earliest mishaps came when two control vessels were put out of action. As they left the transport area to head for the beach, one fouled her screw on a chain buoy and could not go on. The second control vessel continued, only to be suddenly swamped and sunk beneath the cataclysmic cascade of an exploding mine. Another eruption, and an L.C.T. dipped dramatically into the surf.

While this was in progress, the tank-carrying L.C.T.s delayed landing their 32 amphibian tanks until two miles out because of the bad weather. This cut down the risk of swamping from an angry sea three to four miles offshore.

Meanwhile the haze from the bombardment, coupled with the strong tidal conditions and the loss of the control ships, threw the whole operation almost a mile off course. Unaware of this, as the initial assault craft plowed toward their landfall, the

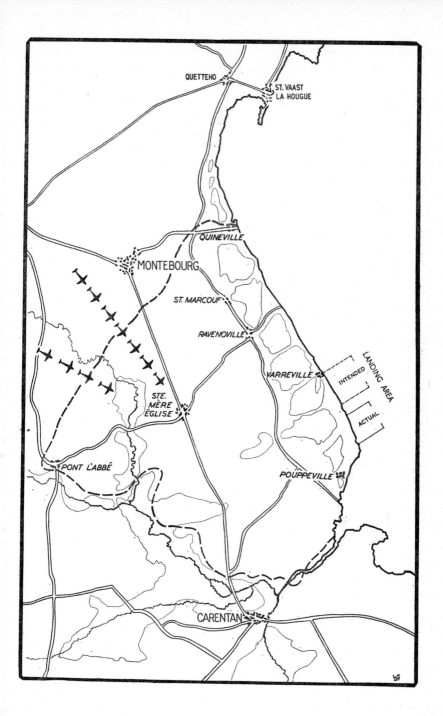

smaller ships still covered them with the bursting barrage from their rocket guns. Some of these support craft now began firing machine guns over the heads of the first assault wave, in the hope that the bullets bouncing on the beach might explode land mines.

Passing minutes and mounting tension. The twenty craft in the first wave arrived at the line of departure on time and advanced abreast. Then when they were 300 to 400 yards from the beach, special smoke projectors signaled the lifting of naval support craft fire. H-Hour had arrived—0630.

Exactly on time, the twenty assault craft lowered their ramps and six hundred men—thirty to each craft—strode into waist-deep water to wade the final hundred yards to the beach.

Now German artillery loosed a few air bursts above the craft, but otherwise opposition was light—luckily. Chewing gum, the GIs waved their rifles as they reached the dry sand.

"Goddam, we're on French soil!" someone shouted.

The eight L.C.T.s, each with four of the DD amphibious tanks, would be in about the same time, while the second and third assault waves were due within fifteen minutes.

Actually the mile error in position now proved an asset, for beach obstacles here were fewer than in the sector planned farther north, and shore defenses here were less formidable than opposite the intended beaches. But with the tide still slightly lower than anticipated, the GIs faced an expanse of open beach that must be crossed before they could scramble to the sand dunes lying low yet inviting at the top of the beach.

This whole side-slip could have been serious, of course, but immediate measures stopped confusion. Brigadier General Theodore Roosevelt rushed to the rear of the beach to check the causeways to be used for the advance. With his aides, he hurried back to the landing points to improvise plans.

Seconds counted. Still there was only a slight pepper of bullets instead of the heavy fire feared.

The casualties came at sea. Enemy guns scored direct hits on two L.C.T.s and sank them. Men struggled in the sea. Weapons dropped to the bottom.

The demolition teams were the men who mattered now. Plans called for eight naval teams to clear fifty-yard gaps in the first band of obstacles. They were due ashore at H+5 minutes. Yes, it was in the water where the danger to the invaders lay. One of the eight craft carrying the demolition men slithered to a stop in the sand at 0635. Just as its ramp thudded down to the water's edge, a German shell shattered the whole bow. Death struck six Americans. One clutched wildly at his head with his hands. Another folded up, almost in half.

Other "obstacle men" jumped into three feet of water carrying their 60 pounds of explosives. Within minutes they blew the first gap at the junction of the beaches, only to find this caused congestion. Craft bunched so dangerously that the men raced on to clear as many gaps as possible quickly.

As the Americans threaded their way up and off the beach, other craft brought in the next waves, and then about a quarter hour later the first eight DD tanks bobbed inshore and once aground trundled out of the sea to lend the infantry close-range support. Their aid proved invaluable and the already reeling German defenders inland fell back before this new vehicle which actually rolled in from the sea firing heavy weapons from the shallows.

Now bulldozers and all manner of vehicles were throbbing up the beach, including a number of Weasels. Major Tabb's vehicle did not stand up to the buffeting water as it left the landing craft, and sank. But Tabb acted promptly and managed to save his crew plus a radio, and made for the beach where he contacted General Roosevelt.

Yet apart from the isolated losses, the expected excitement was missing as more and more specialists sailed in to tackle the beach obstacles. They placed charges by hand against most of them, while the rest were pushed on to the beach by tank bulldozers. Periodic bangs marked the end of these obstacles, only a few of which had mines attached to them. In an hour the entire beach had been cleared, and by the end of its work this force of four hundred men had lost only six killed and thirty-nine wounded.

Obviously the casualties were absurdly low. Could this rate be maintained on all the beaches?

After the engineers forced their way through the mines and all the other paraphernalia, the next obstacle calling for their explosives was the sea wall at the top of the beach. Until it was breached, neither tanks nor other vehicles could leave the quiet but dangerous beach zone. For already the enemy guns inland had got the range of the beach and started shelling. So the engineers blew holes in the wall by the causeway exits and unraveled the coils of barbed wire, as well as piercing paths through the sand dunes. Bangalore torpedoes, mine detectors, explosives and other tools of the trade all opened exits off Utah beach.

Meanwhile, the sun rose and now for a moment it pierced the continuous cloud, throwing sickening shadows beside the few crumpled corpses dotting the water line. And the infantry commenced clearing out houses and enemy garrisons. Some had been so staggered by the bombardment that they did not open fire at all. And all the while, more battalions landed, so that by 0800 four were ashore, and by 1000 two more had waded in. An orderly advance began along the various exits, almost the only alarms being when the infantry waded south through the inundated interiors. The water in this flooded region was normally about waist-deep, but now due to ditches and other odd holes the men frequently tumbled into water over their heads.

Thirteen

Over at Omaha beach the morning made the Utah landings seem like a peacetime beach party. Here hell was the only word to describe what occurred from 0300 onward. In fact from 0251, when headquarters ship *Ancon* anchored in the transport area thirteen miles offshore.

The wind force of 10 to 18 knots caused waves here up to six feet high, while on the beach the breakers measured three to four feet. At this time, 0300, the assault infantry units began to be loaded into their small craft, lowered from parent ships. At once the sea swamped a few, and the pattern was set: a double battle against elements and enemy.

Thus the tragedy of the twenty-nine DD amphibious tanks on the left flank, floundering, foundering, sinking, in the windswept predawn sea. Launched at H−50 minutes from 6,000 yards out, they began to suffer crippling damage within minutes from broken struts, torn canvas, and waters flooding the engine compartments. The remaining three of the thirty-two could not be launched because of a damaged ramp on their L.C.T. As landing craft came within a few miles of the shore, they passed men from the sunken tanks struggling in life preservers and on rafts tossed at the whims of wild waves. Over on the right flank, the DD tanks could not be launched ahead of the assault at all, because of the sea, so the landing craft carrying the infantry had to plod in toward the shore without this vital vanguard support.

Right from the point of departure, spray drenched the assault craft and soon most of them had shipped enough water to need the pumps, which would not carry the load. There was nothing for the troops to do but to bail with their helmets.

Ten out of the 180 to 200 landing craft used in the early waves were definitely swamped, some almost as soon as they were lowered, others nearer the beach, but nearly all the men were saved by naval craft or passing ships.

So from the outset, the troops were drenched again and again, and soon began to suffer from cramps and seasickness as well. But they had been through this sort of training before and many remembered the recent full-dress rehearsal at Slapton Sands, near Dartmouth. One officer thought the whole thing still seemed like another big tactical scheme and could not get the feeling out of his head that it was going to be a miserable two-day job with a hot shower at the end. He could scarcely have been more wrong. For many Americans, nothing was at the end.

Despite all the aids of science in predicting and counteracting wind and current conditions, panoramic photographs, and actual visual beach marks, the entire navigation of the Omaha assault gradually got off course, so that by 0600, craft were coming in anything from a few hundred yards to a mile off course as the unnaturally wild weather inevitably made navigation over thirteen miles inaccurate. What was more, the strong onshore wind whipped the tide higher by half an hour than it would have been normally, so the underwater obstacles were awash sooner than anticipated—and were being hidden deeper every minute. Many men had been seaborne in their little landing craft for three hours now, and had reached a relatively low state of efficiency.

This was the position as H−30 minutes, or rather H−35, brought the bombers on to the scene. From 0555 to 0614 this force of American Liberators added another dramatic disappointment to the lot of the already hard-tried troops. Trying to be sure not to hit any advance craft coming in near the coast, the bombers missed the beach defenses and obstacles altogether. Operating in overcast conditions with a low cloud base, they released their patterns inland instead of in the immediate beach area. This mass attack succeeded in dropping 13,000 fragmentation bombs from a quarter mile to three miles beyond the beaches. Dust drenched the beaches, but that was about all. Although this attack may have smashed much of the German communications, it left the landing craft to face a murderous mortar and shellfire during the final few minutes of their journey.

The concentrated naval barrage broke five minutes before the first bomb fell, at 0550, and continued until H−3 minutes. The battleships *Texas* and *Arkansas* poured some 600 rounds of heavy shells ashore and then came the cruisers, destroyers and support fire. The aim was to neutralize not only the beach defenses but positions which could lay flanking fire on the invasion points. But as with the air assault, the cloud prevented accurate range-finding and the ships had to err on the side of overshooting. It was to prove a costly margin of safety.

The Liberators droned into the distance and sixteen more minutes passed. The naval shells were bursting well behind the beaches still, as the time ticked by on thousands of watches in staccato second hands. More mortar fire was coming from the shore now. And any minute the troops would have to get out of these craft to face the next stage. All along the line the navigational side-slip rippled—from the westerly Dog Green beach, past Dog White and Red, to Easy Green, Easy Red, Fox Green and Fox Red, at the extreme east.

No use relying on anyone now. Some of the tank-landing craft, specially strengthened to allow their self-propelled artillery to fire while still afloat and thus boost the close-support fire, failed to keep their position in the chronic conditions.

Nearer, nearer now. Then 0627, and the overpowering pounding from the ships reached a crescendo of stupendous sound, and abruptly stopped, dead on schedule. Silence for a second. Just three more minutes. Just a few hundred yards of water.

Four hundred and forty yards out, the leading craft came under heavier fire from German automatic weapons and artillery, and even as they did so, the Americans saw that the beaches were unscarred by the air bombardment.

At 0629 men crouched down, clenched their teeth and hands, and waited as that last sixty seconds circled away.

Over on the west flank, directly in front of the draw at Vierville, the tank-landing craft came in. At once the L.C.T. carrying the company commander was hit and sunk just offshore. Five officers were killed or wounded in an instant.

But eight of one company's sixteen tanks got ashore and started to fire from the water's edge.

Now an amphibious tank hit an underwater obstacle in the murky morning and exploded. Nearby a landing craft suffered the same fate, taking a direct hit before its occupants had begun the battle.

One of the six assault landing craft carrying the first infantry wave foundered and began to sink. Well out of their depth, the men had to jump, and Rangers passing in another craft saw them leaping hopelessly from the L.C.A. and being dragged down by their loads. . . .

The assault waves were coming in late. Four to six minutes.

Naught six thirty-five: On Dog Green. A 970-yard strip of hell. The remaining five craft stopped short of the beach, grounding 100 yards out on sand barriers. The automatic weapons had got their range and their fire was actually striking the ramps before they were lowered.

Ramps down: sixteen steps to who knew what. Some of the GIs clattered down and fell into water waist-deep. Others found themselves up to their necks, with their heads targets for the fire from shore. From two particular points, the enemy hit with withering results.

As the range of the ramps attracted a convergence of fire, some of the men dived over the sides or actually kept under the water for as long as they could. Stiff, weak, seasick, and heavily laden, they trudged in through the water, the uneven footing making it all more hellishly slow.

This was twenty minutes in the life—and death—of A Company of the 116th Regiment. 0635—0655. . . .

All boats came under crisscross machine-gun fire. As the first men jumped, they crumpled and flopped into the water. Then order was lost. It seemed to the men that the only way to get ashore was to dive in headfirst and swim clear of the fire that was striking the boats. But as they hit the water, their heavy equip-

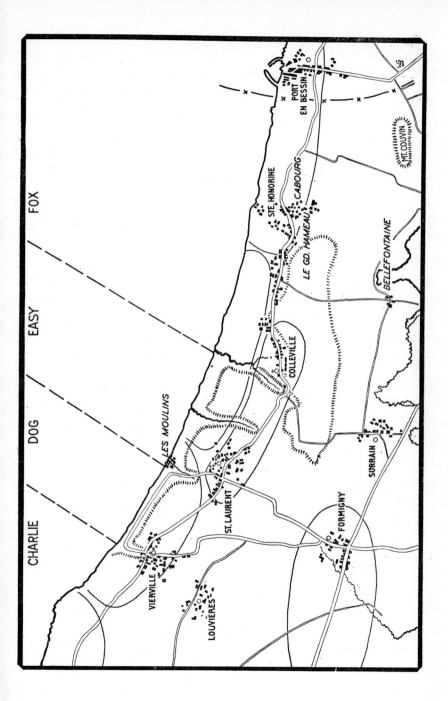

ment dragged them down and soon they were struggling to keep afloat.

Some were hit in the water and wounded. Some drowned. But some moved safely through the bullet fire to the sand and then, finding they could not hold there, went back into the water and used it as cover, remaining with only their heads sticking out. Those who survived kept moving forward with the tide, sheltering at times behind underwater obstacles, and in this way they finally made their landings.

Within ten minutes after the ramps had been lowered, A Company was inert, leaderless and almost incapable of action. Every officer and sergeant had been killed or wounded. It had become a struggle for survival.

The men in the water pushed wounded men ashore ahead of them, and those who had reached the sands crawled back into the water to pull others to land to save them from drowning, in many cases only to see rescued men wounded again or to be hit themselves.

Within twenty minutes of striking the beach, A Company had ceased to be an assault force and had become a forlorn little rescue party bent on survival and the saving of lives.

Meanwhile, mortar fire scored four direct hits on one of the L.C.A.s which literally disintegrated. A Company, or what was left of it, was exhausted when it reached the shore. And the men faced 200 yards of open beach before they could hope for cover from a sea wall or shingle bank.

Darting desultorily from one beach obstacle to another, the men tried to get away. The remnants of one boat team came to try and help, forming a small firing line on the first yards of sand, in full view of the enemy. Despite this heroism, two-thirds of the company were casualties.

H+15. 0645. Two L.C.A.s carried a small U.S. Ranger Company of sixty-four men in to the right of the Vierville draw. An antitank gun got one of the craft, killing a dozen men and shaking up the rest. The other L.C.A. headed on—only to be strafed by a machine gun as the Rangers were halfway down the ramps. Without waiting to organize, the survivors set out across the 250 yards of open sand to the base of a cliff. The time it took to get there: three to four minutes. Mortar and machine guns hit some more men as they advanced. The wounded crawled behind. A few reached the shelter of the cliff, where they took a breath and a count—thirty-five men lost, twenty-nine left.

The Rangers faced the fiercest onslaught of all on this right flank. Storming ashore in face of one of the few exits from Omaha— actually opposite Vierville—another company met the fatal fury of at least two German strongpoints covering the road through the place.

Gripping their guns in both hands, they jumped off the ramps, one or two actually being hit in midair and never reaching dry land. Others crouched, crawled or raced toward the only shelter of a sea wall. Men met the murderous inferno of fire from all land sides. This was it. The moment of truth, life, death.

And their only chance—the wall. Some staggered through the shallows, others aimed across the beach for it diagonally. And all the time the hail of bullets went on.

Someone fell, hit. A wrecked craft drifted crazily broadside onto the shore, its job done. A Ranger lay face down in a pool of water, stained red.

One hundred and thirty Rangers landed here. Sixty-two survived to reach the sea wall. Less than half.

Why was the defense so strong? Unluckily the enemy troops in the area had only just been augmented by a field formation which happened to be holding a stand-to exercise on the coast and manned the defenses as the Allied assault began.

The rest of the 116th came in past poles and spikes sticking alarmingly out of the water, but luck was on their side. Company G landed more than half a mile east of their intended Dog White beach, on Dog Red, where the earlier barrage had started grass fires. Smoke from these created a complete screen between the beach and the defenses, shrouding their vulnerable position from the bluff beyond. Not stopping to query their fortune, the men scampered across the tidal flat, relieved that the smoke was still sufficiently dense to stop the almost continuous line of enemy emplacements from zeroing in on them. If the barrage had not knocked out many of the defenses, at least it had laid an unintentional smoke screen. The GIs were halfway up the flat before any firing at all reached them, and then it remained inaccurate, causing only a few casualties.

Much heavier fire met the other sections of the company, which lost fourteen men on Easy Green.

F Company hit the beaches right in front of the fortified Les Moulins. Three sections also on Easy Green were shattered by concentrated fire from various weapons and it was not until three-quarters of an hour later that they had got across the exposed expanse of sand. By then half were dead or wounded, and the rest in no state for assault action.

At the same time as A and F Companies were plunging into the pain and eternity of Dog Green and Easy Green, the rest of the regiment hit beaches farther east, earmarked for the 16th Regiment, to be hit by more fire at almost point-blank range.

Men of E Company were put out in waist-deep water, but hit a deep trough as they waded in and had to swim through surf and strong currents which bore them east. Flamethrowers, mortars, bazookas and small arms were all dropped in the struggle for survival. Yet when the men finally dripped breathlessly ashore they dragged themselves up to the sheltering shingle to find they had lost only two men from enemy fire.

A little to the left, a drifting section of F Company unloaded in neck-deep water and seventeen men out of thirty-one died on the way to the shingle. On the whole of the mile-wide stretch of Easy Red, these four sections were the sum total of assault elements for the first half hour—except for four DD tanks which survived the weather. And one of these was soon struck leaving only three.

On to the Fox beaches and the other American assault regiment —the 16th. Here craft scattered badly over a front of 800 yards, thus weakening their power-through-concentration. Although the final run-in did not incur many losses, crossfire caught the craft exactly as the ramps went splashing down. Bullets seared into the men as they jumped. And as others stopped to drag the wounded ashore, they too were hit in the water. Soaked uniforms hung heavily on them; soaked, wounded men weighed still heavier; and by the time they scraped their way to the beach—still 300 yards from the shingle bank—all they could do was crawl in ahead of the tide. Most of the company's 105 casualties for the day came between 0630 and 0700.

Stray sections of E Company, 116th Regiment, bobbed in on the same shore where their commander, Captain Laurence Madill, staggered across the beach wounded. Weaker each second, he returned to the water's edge to try to salvage mortar ammunition. Machine-gun bullets hit him twice more.

As he reeled round and fell his last words were:

"Senior noncom, take the men off the beach."

Mortars and machine guns combined to take a toll of one in every three men as F Company landed in front of enemy strong-points.

Just as the right and center assaults aimed at Vierville and St. Laurent, the left struck for Colleville following the Americans' strategy of head-down, head-on battering attack, at the precise points where the enemy were likely to be strongest. The morning would decide on the wisdom of such strategy, but it looked as if it would be a lesson learned dearly in terms of human life.

So at Easy Red and Fox Green, on either side of the Colleville exit, exactly the same stark scene seemed to be recurring as at Dog Green.

Over on the east, men swept in by the surf landed soaking and swearing under the very guns flanking the exit. Into the valley of death.

Some of the craft sank before they even headed in toward Fox Green. Others were hit by shells on the run-in. One shell exploded right in the middle of the men in a crowded craft.

But somehow, despite the surf and the shells, they came in, late and out of place but still at Omaha on that memorable morning. None of them living now would have missed it. Thankfully the general drag east had pushed many of them just far enough away from Fox Green to have a chance. Seeing the battering bursts of fire from this area, the American commanders now modified the original head-on dash and struck out east towards

Port en Bessin. This was the place adjacent to Arromanches where they were due to link up with the British.

The cliffs starting east from Fox Green helped to shield this movement and thus the debacle of Dog Green was not repeated. But it was bad enough, although the supporting destroyers and rocket craft stood close inshore, in vulnerable waters, to try and cover the movement off the beach.

Abruptly a salvo of sheets of flame spat at an angle into the air, announcing the opening fire from a rocket craft: a volley equal to the firing power of 200 destroyers! And these craft could come in closer than destroyers. It was a breath-taking, breath-holding barrage.

I Company lost a couple of craft swamped, and ended up far east of the Fox beaches. L Company was luckiest of all. Artillery hit a landing craft a few seconds after the last man left it, and one of its sections showed that a successful landing without casualties was possible by spreading out widely to move up the beach without losing a single man. In fact, L Company was the only one of the eight in the first assault to be ready to operate as a unit after crossing the lethal lower beaches.

With these first forces went a special engineer task force to tackle beach obstacles. Delays in loading and the wholesale mis-handlings meant that half of the sixteen teams of engineers reached shore ten minutes or more late. And at least three teams landed where there were neither infantry nor tanks to cover them with protective fire. Men loaded with equipment and explosives staggering through several feet of water presented sitting targets.

Only six of sixteen bulldozers beached in working order, and enemy artillery at once hit three of these six.

Eight naval engineers were dragging the preloaded rubber boat off their landing craft when a shell burst just above their load of explosives. One of the eight lived. . . .

A mortar shell struck another rubber boat full of explosives as the men pulled it through the surf. Amazingly, four were only wounded.

Over on a landing craft, a shell fell squarely on the deck and detonated, killing everyone on board.

Finally, as one craft came toward the shallows a shell struck the ramp, hurling three men into the water. The craft drifted out of control until another shell caught her full on the bow. Fifteen men died.

Yet despite these disasters, the engineers went on—and actually got to work on those deadly beaches. One of the three bulldozers left had to postpone its maneuvers to stop and give shelter to hard-pressed infantrymen. Every clang of a bullet against the bulldozer meant a possible life saved.

Yes, the engineers were working in impossible difficulties. One team was all ready to blow a lane through the beach obstacles when a landing craft came hurtling up on a wave, crashed into the obstacles and set off seven mines. Another team laid their charges for a thirty-yard gap and was just skipping back to take cover when a mortar shell struck the primer cord. The premature explosion killed or wounded nineteen engineers.

But in their allotted time they blew six gaps all along the Omaha front, although owing to loss of equipment only one could be marked so that the other five were of less use at high tide.

Most of the high proportion of 41 per cent casualties to engineers were sustained in that first half hour trying to clear a way for the second wave.

Fourteen

NOUGHT seven hundred—and the scene on Dog Green was repeated as the second wave touched down in a series of landings lasting forty minutes. The remnants of A Company were still staggering under the shock of those first twenty-five minutes as B Company bottomed. By now, too, the tide had flowed right into the obstacle belt—and through it by 0800—and the beach obstacles were not yet gapped in many places. No one had advanced beyond the shingle; tanks were unable to give much covering fire; and the tide would rise eight feet in the next hour. It was not a bright prospect.

By luck, only a small part of the three companies actually landed on Dog Green where the same shattering crossfire decimated their strength in a matter of minutes. Everything was happening in minutes; seconds, even. Yet seconds could seem eternities. A machine-gun burst stabbed the line of the tide, its bullets throwing up spurts of spray before reaching and riddling a wounded GI as he hung on to an underwater obstacle. The same destructive fire pinned B Company to the water's edge.

Some of the craft were saved by the tide as the wind drove it and the boats a little to the left. Behind the cover of a providential pall of smoke, these men now got across the open beach to the blind side of a sea wall and, overcoming all obstacles, wire and mines, penetrated inland.

Following ten minutes behind B Company, C came in at 0710 at the west end of Dog White. One of its six craft got off to a bad, if not fatal, start by running right into a mined obstacle. For twenty frantic minutes, its crew maneuvered in the surf to get it free without setting off the mines! Only one other suffered

137

setback: the sea threw it against a ramp and it capsized, spilling the men into five feet of water and causing them to lose all their precious flamethrowers and charges.

Still the sea claimed as many casualties as the enemy. Three of D Company's six craft shipped water badly and one had to be abandoned before the invasion had begun.

Four hundred yards out, another one suddenly sank in the surf, and the men scrambled into the water, struggling to swim for shore under a blinding barrage of mortar shells and bullets. About half of them reached the damp sands.

Yet another section disembarked a long way out and saw riflemen lying full-length in the shallows, sheltering behind the steel X obstacles. The scattered survivors eventually got ashore but their total arms consisted of one mortar and no ammunition.

So it went on. Battalion Headquarters and Headquarters Company came in on time, but when the landing crafts' ramps went down the fire was so intense that many men took refuge behind some tanks only to find these the targets of heavy artillery fire.

Later, Major Sidney Bingham, Jr., battalion commander, tried to organize an assault on Les Moulins, but so many of the fifty men he gathered had rifles clogged with sand that it was impossible for them really to build up any volume of fire!

Now the reinforcements arrived thick and fast. Tired and cramped, they were glad that the German fire had slackened a little, for as one of them put it:

"The burdens we ordinarily carried, we had to drag."

Still machine-gun bullets kicked up the sand, but the men took shelter and discovered that the guns were delivering fixed fire, so they could advance along routes which avoided the bullets.

Yet some fire was inevitable. Losses were low here, for in the words of a survivor, "It's surprising how much small-arms fire a man can run through without getting hit."

Lighter losses generally were the rule for the later assault waves. Some men were shielded by burning grass, but actually the decrease in casualties was probably due more to the fact that as the landings increased, the enemy had to spread their attention to more formations. As the main command group beached about

138

0730, one craft knocked a Teller mine off its perch without any explosion! The Germans' fire from the bluffs was masked by smoke.

Meanwhile back on the original beach, the Germans were being disturbed by fire from Allied destroyers and smaller craft that had witnessed the reception to A Company. Defying both opposition and the risk of running aground, these ships swung gamely toward the Dog Green beach to bring their guns to bear on the two strong-points still dangerous to the Americans. Eventually their fire took effect, and the troops were able to regroup on the beach behind any cover they could. They were even able to get a line out to a couple of colleagues wounded and wading ashore from landing craft which had been wrecked and lay low in the shallows as the waves broke over it. Thankfully the men grabbed the rope and were hauled up to the beach by men up to the knees in water. Quickly one and all dispersed and only the landing craft remained.

Fierce fighting went on all along the beaches. The four-mile stretch of Omaha beach was well covered at either end by sheer 100-foot cliffs. Now the main German crossfire was coming from the bluff overlooking the western sector, and from the central exit point at which the American landings had been aimed. On top of all this there were still mines, wire obstructions and ditches to be overcome.

Engineers were still working furiously as the second assault waves of the 16th Regiment bumped over the sand barriers off Easy Red and through the thick obstacles. There was another reason for losses now. The cramped, heavily laden troops could only advance at walking pace: they physically could not run. Enemy snipers picked many off as they made the uphill trek off the lower beach. Nevertheless they had their supporting weapons working within a quarter of an hour.

Bullets, swamping, fire, mines, artillery shells, still the pattern of sound and fury kept up its cacophony. One craft got itself hung up on an obstacle and a German machine gun poured fire into it at will until its occupants were all dead.

The smoke screen of burning grass in the center sector was having its effect on the Americans, as well as protecting them. They were well east of their appointed place, and they could

139

scarcely distinguish any landmarks or a way through the mine fields. Inevitably, the beaches became more crowded, with no exits yet available. German guns managed to penetrate the gloom through gaps in the smoke, and soon their shells started exploding around the later landing craft and vehicles. Plenty of troops were coming ashore, but they could do little constructive without exits.

The first hour was over when one of the worst disasters of the day occurred. L.C.I. 91 was approaching Dog White at 0740 with the alternative headquarters of the 116th Regiment. Artillery fire hit it on its first attempt to get through the obstacles. Backing out, the vessel came in for a second try, but the tide had flooded high now and Element C was scarcely showing. The L.C.I. could not get through, so the ramps were dropped in deep water. As the officers led the way down in six or seven feet of water, an artillery shell fell right on the crowded forward deck, sending up a sheet of flame. Burning, screaming men jumped or fell into the sea, struggling to swim ashore under continuing artillery fire.

As if this were not enough tragedy, L.C.I. 92 came into the same sector a few minutes later and suffered almost as badly. It struck a mine and its fuel tanks exploded and burst into scorching fire which burned for hours after the last man had jumped to escape roasting.

Conditions were chronic for landing the vehicles now arriving. If the jeeps, trucks and other vehicles managed to get close enough to avoid deep water, and unloading in surf under fire, they found they were on strips of sand which narrowed hourly and from which there were no exits. The traffic jam began.

One battalion lost 28 of its 36 machine guns, while water and sand made other guns unusable. Colonel Canham reported three-quarters of the 116th's radios useless.

Meanwhile, before their very eyes, the rising tide was drowning wounded men stranded on the edge of the water. Stunned and shaken by that first hour, the men were glad of the apparent safe cover of the sea wall and shingle bank. They had no wish to go on at present. But some officers saw the danger of this. Morale was low. If they were not careful, they would be open to a counter-attack before they had got off the beaches.

140

Even at Easy Red, where the resistance was lighter, the Germans were preventing the 16th from leaving the beach. The GIs got across the firm sand, gray-brown under the ominous scudding clouds, but then the beach banked up steeply into a shingle ridge. Beyond this were wire obstacles. A steady fire forced them to keep their heads down.

The decisive factor proved to be—leadership. Where did they go from there? No one could see how it was possible to advance straight over the top. Then on Easy Red a young lieutenant and an already wounded sergeant suddenly stood up, disregarding the frequent firing, and calmly walked over to look at the wire beyond the embankment. Somehow they were not hit. The lieutenant returned and, hands on hips, looked down at the men lying behind the shingle.

"Are you going to lay there and get killed, or get up and do something about it?" he called across to them.

None of them moved, so with the sergeant he got the group's explosives, walked back to the obstacles and blasted a way through the wire. At last the men stirred, and the lieutenant led the way single file and under continuous fire up a path prickling with mines. Thus, slowly, they got to grips with the enemy defenses which covered the beach. Another company landed and followed the same route. But now they faced the double danger of shelling and the mines. Shells burst nearby, yet they dare not stop nor lie down. The mine menace was everywhere. One moment a man would be trudging up the path; the next, a blinding burst, and his pal in front lay huddled ahead of him. And all he could do was walk around what was left.

The remnants of an isolated section of B Company of the 116th were stopped early by fire from a well-concealed emplacement. The lieutenant in charge went after it single-handed. But in the act of tossing a grenade into the rifle pit, he was hit by three bullets and eight grenade fragments, including some from his own grenade. He clutched himself and fell, but not before turning his map and compass over to a sergeant and ordering the group to press on inland.

While the second wave was being bundled ashore from a fierce sea into a fiercer shore, three companies of U.S. Rangers—or American Commandos—had to assault the sheer cliff face of Pointe du Hoe three miles off Dog Green. And to do it they had the Wheezers and Dodgers' cliff-scaling gear they had tested on the Isle of Wight. The aim was to neutralize a battery believed to be located on top of the cliff which could fire on either of the two American assault areas—O and U. Six 155-mm. howitzers were understood to be in the battery.

As the cliff rose a sheer 85 to 100 feet high, the ten assault landing craft carried three rocket guns apiece which fired grapnels which in turn pulled up plain ropes, toggle ropes, and rope ladders. Each craft also carried tubular steel extension ladders, while four DUKWs mounted a 100-foot extension ladder.

Companies E and F were scheduled to scale the east side of the point, and D Company the west, with the landings to take place at H-Hour, 0630. Unluckily, the general east drift also affected the Rangers' craft. One of the ten L.C.A.s was swamped soon after leaving the transport area, while further trouble came from the supply boats: one sank and the second had to jettison all packs to stay afloat. A small gun in a cliff position sank one of the DUKWs, but the nine surviving L.C.A.s sailed in under covering fire from two destroyers, whose guns lobbed shells all over the area beyond the battery. At H-Hour the barrage was lifted and the craft had to go on alone, but the destroyer *Satterlee* spotted the Germans recovering to man clifftop trenches, so she swept the place for a final time with her guns.

Despite this, as the craft beached over half an hour late—and all on the east side—scattered fire knocked out fifteen Rangers on the heavily cratered shore.

Immediately on touch down, the Rangers fired their rockets over the cliff, only to have many fail to carry with the water-soaked ropes. Nor could the DUKWs get across the cratered beach, so their ladders were not much use.

Germans appeared peering down over the cliff and started to harass the Rangers with occasional rifle fire and grenades which merely had to be lobbed down. But the Rangers picked off these snipers as soon as they exposed themselves on the skyline, and

142

the *Satterlee* swung in close to strafe the clifftop a second time with all her guns.

One or two ropes either were cut by the enemy at the top, or slipped from their anchorage, but in less than five minutes after touch down the first Rangers bobbed to the top. Others followed, walking almost horizontally up the cliff. Below, the beach and rocks looked miniature. Ahead they might encounter the enemy any minute. It was not a pleasant place to linger.

Up there on the top they found a no man's land with all landmarks destroyed and the ground so cratered by the naval shells that if they got even five yards apart they lost contact. The few Germans they saw quickly went underground in a network of mined dugouts. Operating according to rehearsals, the GIs split up to head for the gun positions, only to find them wrecked and the guns removed.

Pairs of Rangers fanned out at once to search for the secret spot hiding the battery, when they came under heavy fire from the south. They pushed on nevertheless and wiped out two nests of resistance, though not before losing fifteen men killed or wounded. Then they regrouped and took up defensive positions while preparing again to look for the missing battery.

Meanwhile down at the foot of the cliff things were happening. By 0730 all the Ranger boat teams were ashore, and by 0740 all were up the cliff. Then just west of the Point an anti-aircraft gun started sweeping the area with fire, so a dozen of the boat teams were sent to attack the position. Suddenly the Germans, driven to ground by the first assault of Rangers, emerged from their tunnels and trenches and overwhelmed eleven of the twelve men. The one man to escape stumbled back through the craters to the command post to tell the news and another assault was improvised on the site. The Rangers got just halfway to the strongpoint when artillery fire pounded down on the party, killing or wounding practically every man there.

Back inland, the Rangers resumed their patrols at once, and about 0900 two of them came on the missing battery situated down a lane off the main road. Cleverly camouflaged, the five guns

143

were situated so they could fire on either Omaha or Utah beaches and had plentiful stocks of ammunition. But no crews!

So the patrol of two Rangers wasted no time in case the Germans appeared, and destroyed two of the guns with incendiary grenades. While they returned for more grenades, they summoned a second patrol who polished off the job of disabling the guns and firing the ammunition. A pair of Rangers had put the most potentially deadly enemy emplacement facing the entire American sectors of the invasion out of action.

In case the command post did not guess by the deafening explosions, word was sent back to the Point that the main mission had been accomplished. And meanwhile the small force at the Point were in something like a siege. Gradually they cleaned out the Germans in that incredible maze of craters and trenches, although it was a slow business. The only signal which the commander, Colonel Rudder, could send was:

"Located Pointe du Hoe—mission accomplished—need ammunition and reinforcement—many casualties."

Down on Dog White the assault of the bluffs began. It was an uphill struggle in every way. The officers were wonderful. Colonel Canham held up an injured wrist but went on with his work. General Cota walked up and down behind the sea wall urging men of the 116th to get moving. Private Ingram Lambert was one who responded. He jumped over the wall, crossed the road, and set a Bangalore torpedo to clear a path. But a bullet from a machine gun killed him, the friction igniter on the torpedo failed to act, and Second Lieutenant Stanley Schwartz went over and fixed it. The explosive blew a big gap in the double-apron wire entanglement. The first man of the platoon to advance through the gap fell shot, but others followed and got through. Captain Berthier Hawks, who had suffered a crushed foot in the landing, got to the top of the bluff with his men of Company C.

A Ranger formation joined C Company at the same time. In the smoke, though, they scarcely knew anyone else was in that area. As they advanced they had to wear gas masks against the smoke. When they reached the top, too, they discovered the Germans had left so quickly they had not even struck their signs

144

work all over Britain, another group was threading a tortuous way through the mines. They cut the wire successfully and started their job. Every second this day there was the smell of smoke and sound of shells, mortars, or machine guns punctuating and almost numbing their thoughts. Now mines, too. The leading platoon gingerly plodded forward. Dust from the dunes blew inland with the wind.

The first bang came, followed by a second. A third. But now there was no panic. There could be no way back to the beaches. They had to get through. Their bridges burned behind, they faced mines ahead and on each flank. A corporal clutched his face wildly as one mine blew itself to bits. A private stepped just beside one—and it ripped his leg apart. Fumes from the explosive stank. Everywhere it was the same and now thin lines of wounded men marked the way: men who dare not move a muscle for fear of firing another one. But a gap had to be made, a way paid for by their own lives if necessary. And at last they were through.

Along Fox Green, north of Colleville, the second assault lines had snaked ashore across the beach, being hit hard on the way. Yet by 0800 an assault started up the rises, and on Fox Red where the bluff merged into a partial cliff. At this eastern end of Omaha, tanks were rumbling up the sloping beach and the commander of L Company, 16th Regiment, stood up to direct their fire onto enemy resistance points. He was at once shot dead.

Another section of this company got to the top of the hill but had to stop suddenly and telephone the beach, because fire from one of their own destroyers was focused on an enemy strongpoint only a little way ahead—and they had no wish to be hit by their own guns after having survived the ordeal of the beaches. As soon as the naval fire ceased, the Americans stormed the strongpoint. Half the thirty German prisoners taken were wounded.

Other small isolated assaults were going on all along the front, from the extreme west beach beyond Dog Green—designated Charlie. Rangers surviving the blaze of beach tracer and mortar fire found themselves stuck at the base of a 90-foot cliff which was impossible to climb. They moved carefully still further west and 300 yards away found a crevice in the slope. Using bayonets for successive hand holds in the cliff, and pulling each other up, they grasped and gasped their way toward the top, monkey-walking the last part with toggle ropes attached to stakes in an enemy mine-field near the crest!

The penetrations made in the period up to 1000 hours could not be followed up properly because the engineers were still working under so many difficulties—so that at 0800 no gaps yet existed in the shingle. Yet vehicles continued to arrive and threatened to clog the beaches still under artillery fire, so that about 0830 vehicle landings were suspended temporarily. The Cannon Company of the 16th got its halftrack tanks ashore but could not move them more than 50 yards through the litter of disabled vehicles. Its six howitzers loaded on DUKWs never fired, for one by one the DUKWs were swamped with the loss of twenty men drowned. The artillery, too, were suffering. One group was immobilized as soon as it landed. A battalion commander soon saw they could never operate guns in those conditions and decided to make the best of it:

"To hell with our artillery mission. We've got to be infantrymen now."

Colonel Mullins lived up to his words and although twice wounded went to work organizing little groups of infantry. Next he led a tank forward to direct its fire on an emplacement. The point was hit. He ran across an open stretch toward another tank, but never reached it.

The DUKWs seemed to be far from justifying their name, for five more were swamped, and a further four lost when circling the rendezvous area: one of them turned turtle as they started the run-in; another stopped with engine trouble and became a "sitting duck"; and the last pair got close enough to see that there was nowhere possible to land, stopped to talk it over, and were promptly set afire. Eight men swam ashore safely.

And still the heartbreaking losses to vital vehicles continued. Three L.C.T.s struck mines at high tide. One capsized into seven feet of water, while on another a howitzer had to be jettisoned with a huge splash to keep the craft afloat.

The tanks which did get ashore had a rough time, trapped

between high water and the embankments, a good target for the guns on the bluffs. The commander of the 741st Tank Company came aground at 0820 but salt water got into his radio so the command group had to run up and down the bullet-swept stretches contacting their tanks. Three of the five men were killed in the process. At the other end of Omaha, the commander of the 743rd Tank Company, Lieutenant Colonel John Upham, was shot down as he walked over to a tank.

Nevertheless the tanks kept on firing. One disabled tank kept its guns blazing while the water got deeper and deeper around and eventually drowned them out. An infantry battalion commander said soon afterward:

"The tanks saved the day. They shot the hell out of the Germans, and got the hell shot out of them."

Dozens of different actions went on every minute. Naval fire was beginning to help the troops now. And landing ships were developing bolder techniques to tackle the now nearly submerged obstacles. L.C.T. 30 drove at full speed through them, all weapons firing. L.C.I. 544 also rammed her way through the obstacles while actually accounting for an enemy machine-gun nest in a fortified house. A barrage balloon broken adrift flew crazily surveying this scene three hours after the first troops had hit land.

Nought nine thirty-five: to a waiting world that knew nothing, communiqué No. 1 was issued by Supreme H.Q., Allied Expeditionary Force, announcing the opening of the Second Front.

"Under the command of General Eisenhower, Allied naval forces, supported by strong air forces, began landing Allied armies this morning on the northern coast of France."

Within minutes, Britain and occupied Europe heard the news.

Yet at this precise moment, the commanders were actually having to consider diverting part of Force Omaha through the British Force Gold Beaches, an emergency measure that eventually was not necessary.

This was a turning point: too many vehicles, too few combat troops. The earlier waves were dug in to the shelter of the sand, but the beaches were still subjected to the deafening fire which pinned them there.

Too few troops—and too few exits. How had it happened that the Americans found themselves faced with such a crisis which, if it did not jeopardize the whole Operation Overlord, certainly left the success of the western half of the assault in doubt?

First: since the assault craft had been lowered some twelve miles out, on a night when an onshore wind sent the sea streaming coastward, the danger of swamping and the difficulty of navigating were naturally increased.

As Admiral Ramsay records with typical British understatement: "In the rough weather that obtained when the assault forces arrived in the lowering positions, the longer passage inshore for the assault craft from the Western Task Force appeared to add appreciably to their difficulties."

Second: the Americans instead of landing where the beach defenses were weakest aimed to land right in front of the natural exits from the beaches and storm the strongpoints covering them—although the major German fortifications were concentrated opposite these beach exits.

Third: the Americans rejected Montgomery's plan to land heavy armor accompanied by all the specially developed equipment designed for overcoming obstacles at the start of the attack. Without flail tanks, flame-throwing tanks and anti-obstacle armored vehicles, the Americans were left with the flotation-gear DD tanks, and when these could not swim ashore as planned, all the 1st Division had were bulldozers. Meanwhile the heavily harassed U.S. Engineers were gamely trying to neutralize pillboxes with polecharges; to smash their way through barbed wire and thick concrete walls with packets of explosives which they actually had to position by hand while they were as often as not being fired on from beyond the obstacles.

They were the first to agree with Colonel Taylor to "get the hell out of here" but the question was still how—and where?

Fifteen

BETWEEN four and five in the morning, the first landing craft of the British and Canadian Eastern Task Force were lowered from their parent ships or slipped tows some eight miles offshore along a line between Arromanches in the west to Ouistreham to the east. Allied airborne forces had already been fighting for several hours over on the mainland, and even now the American craft lowered further out to sea from Utah and Omaha were having a rough time of it.

Here in the Gold, Juno and Sword sectors, the weather was just as bad. Gone was the watery-blue sunset someone remembered in the Solent a day or two before, and in its place was just the wind and the waves. Above the wind at that unlikely hour men heard a bugler somewhere actually sounding the general salute. Then they were on their own in tiny crowded craft buffeted by four-foot-high waves. Some of the ships making their way across under their own steam had been forced to return. Others kept at it. L.C.A. 712 had been damaged by the sea soon after leaving the Isle of Wight area, but chugged on across the Channel until the time came to slip her tow. This caused more trouble, with the tug vessel and the L.C.A. rising and falling at different moments, and generally being blown into each other. At last it was accomplished, however, although later they were to learn how insignificant their troubles had been before.

All through that night crammed craft had been moving slowly in long columns, shepherded by such ships as corvettes which would dash up alongside with land-hailers. Now in the night's gloom, the blue and camouflage colors were unseen.

Lorries and armored vehicles jolted about on the Rhino craft

151

ferries, some of which snapped their tows to add to the confusion. Rifles and Sten guns slung over the rest of their kit, the men sat and rested and thought—or were sick into the special bags issued for the purpose.

Nought four forty-five: the Merville battery won. They were nearer now to the shore.

Everyone in the DD tanks' units was up early for final water-proofing and sealing to the waders. Breakfast even, and radio sets to be warmed up. Launching drill to be dress rehearsed for the DD tanks.

Over on an infantry-landing craft they swung and tossed in the flat-bottomed boat. They issued all the bundles of maps and at last they learned the proper names of their destination: Lion-sur-Mer. They knew they would be aiming for a gabled-end house—if it were still standing. Few managed to eat breakfast. Most had been violently sick, despite the boiled sweets and cups of tea.

Nought five fifteen: bombardment time. This was the precise planned hour when the leading landing craft would come in range of the German coastal defenses—if they could be seen so far out at sea on such a misty dawn.

So to the accompaniment of a supporting air attack, the British navy opened fire forty minutes before sunrise. From H.M.S. *Arethusa* off the Orne, to the 6-inch guns of H.M.S. *Ajax* facing the famous beaches of Arromanches. *Ajax* engaged the only one of the enemy's heavy coastal batteries which retaliated to the bombardment—at Longues, between the British and American sectors. Fire from other enemy batteries at La Rivière and Ouistreham ignored the advancing landing craft to concentrate on the capital ships—too far out to be in much danger of direct hits. The German fire was largely ineffective due also to the continuing air assault—inaccurate as it inevitably was in the conditions—and the Allied measures to prevent the Germans from ranging and spotting. Credit for successful spotting in connection with our naval barrage went to the pilots of single-seater fighter aircraft who flew to and fro over that dawn invasion coast line reporting the range and results of the ship's guns.

Just as on the American front, this murderous assault built up

152

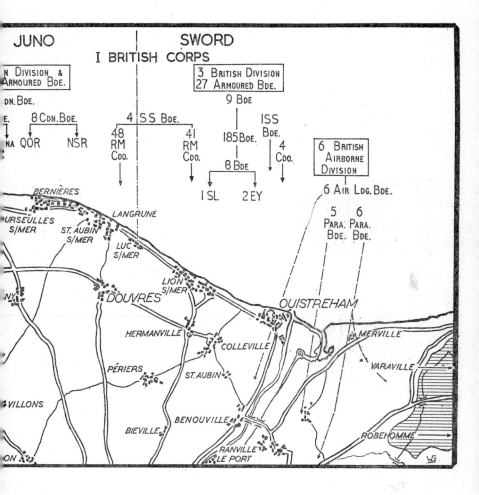

JUNO   SWORD

I BRITISH CORPS

N DIVISION &
ARMOURED BDE.

DN. BDE.

E.
NA   QOR   NSR
8 CDN. BDE.

4 SS BDE.

3 BRITISH DIVISION
27 ARMOURED BDE.

9 BDE

ISS
BDE.

48
RM
CDO.

41
RM
CDO.

185 BDE.

4
CDO.

8 BDE

6 BRITISH
AIRBORNE
DIVISION

1 SL   2 EY

6 AIR LDG. BDE.

5   6
PARA. PARA.
BDE. BDE.

BERNIERES

URSEULLES
S/MER

ST. AUBIN
S/MER

LANGRUNE

LUC
S/MER

LION
S/MER

DOUVRES

OUISTREHAM

MERVILLE

HERMANVILLE

COLLEVILLE

VARAVILLE

PÉRIERS

ST. AUBIN

VILLONS

BENOUVILLE

BIEVILLE

ROBEHOMME

RANVILLE
LE PORT

Meanwhile the imposing tank-landing craft could see shells from the Western Task Force bursting to the south. Although the wind had dropped, the sea remained rough at force 5, too rough for the amphibious tanks. Thus as it became lighter and the time for launching the DDs neared, they anxiously awaited the signal from Brigadier Prior-Palmer on the headquarters ship which would tell them to "swim or not to swim" the tanks.

"Floater 5,000."

The signal came shortly before 0630 and meant that the distance for the tanks to be swum had been shortened to 5,000 yards. Quickly the L.C.T.s closed to this distance, less than three miles from Sword beach, opposite Lion-sur-Mer. The big craft came into line, anchored, and in a strong wind blowing now from the west, started to launch the two squadrons of amphibious tanks— twenty DD Shermans to each squadron. All the L.C.T.s except one launched their tanks well despite the sea as the naval supporting fire strengthened.

Most of the forty tanks got off to a good start after the launching. In the one craft not lucky in launching, L.C.T. 467, carrying the B Squadron leader, the first tank tore its canvas and could not launch, thus blocking the way for the others in the craft. Major Rugge-Price wanted to jettison the tank but was overruled and the L.C.T. was eventually beached late.

L.C.T. 465 launched four of its five DD tanks according to plan but the fourth broke the chains of the ramp door as it descended —so the fifth tank had to be carried back to England.

One of the tanks in A Squadron suffered ill luck, too, its propellers failing to engage the water. In the sweeping surf, the tank could make no headway and was soon overcome by the waves and sank. As it went down, however, the crew inflated their rubber dinghy and pitched into it, to be rescued.

Once the tanks were in the water, things went well. They picked up their pilot boats and the columns steered steadily for the beach in good formation. They had never experienced so rough a sea in training, yet the tanks stood up to it all. Now that it was full light they could see the dramatic display of the barrage bursting among the houses on the sea front, and the fighter bombers racing up and down dangerously low over the beach. Some of the rockets from the ships were falling very short now and Lieutenant Burgess in one DD was hit by a splinter and later died from the wound.

With the assault landing craft, close beside the unarmed vessels came the formidable rocket landing craft. Moving in closer than destroyers, cruisers and other support ships, the rocket carriers loosed searing salvos on every possible point ashore. Each salvo equaled the whole destroyer strength of the Royal Navy: a sobering thought. The hiss of their rocket banks fizzed far over the waters as they rounded rapidly to get in position again.

Through the glasses the Warwickshires could see their gabled-end house—and the spouts of shooting water as shells from both sides fell into the sea. Black and white smoke on the beaches. One or two Messerschmitts now, and two landing craft actually hit by bombs. Another struck a mine, but most of them got through. Funny whining noises now. Their first enemy fire. Thumping chests and a deep sinking feeling in their stomachs.

And with the Eastern Task Force sailed 45 Hedgerows—those tows of mortars for countermining the beaches and breaching as many shore defenses as they could by sheer blast.

Like other assault landing craft, the L.C.A.s carrying the Hedgerows could barely cope with the sea conditions encountered on the run-in, and of one flotilla of nine, all except one L.C.A. sank. Most of the Hedgerow craft came through, though, including L.C.A. 712 whose tribulations began the previous day. Lined up on its assault station after the trouble with the tow, it was just being prepared for firing when a 6-inch shell shattered its armored doors. Despite this and heavy small-arms fire, the commander continued with the attack and saw his salvo of bombs explode halfway up the beach.

Ill equipped for such seas, the L.C.A.s often found themselves nearly flooded from the surf, and No. 1071 shipped a lot of water. Its tow also parted before the arranged time, but it aimed toward its target—a gap in the sea wall filled with sandbags and overlooked by a greenhouse. Holding on his course, the commanding officer suddenly swerved to avoid the top of an obstacle popping out of the tide, and fired his Hedgerow. As he turned, he saw the bombs burst in and beyond the wall. At once, heavy small-arms fire from the house riddled their ensign, but as the wall was breached he headed toward the parent ship. The sea still threatened to capsize the craft, but he got it back and was hoisted inboard.

L.C.A. 876 went so close that she almost ran aground as she fired her bombs, which blew a tremendous breach in the sea wall. Other Hedgerow craft fired Teller mines beneath the beaches and on the Gold sector especially, these pre-assault salvos helped the men to land later.

All along the line, the craft were getting nearer the beach now, and the sea was more and more filled with vessels of every kind.

Nought seven ten: Sea mines, too, had to be avoided. Dead ahead of an L.C.A. a moored mine bobbed above the surf. The helmsman heaved the wheel with all his strength. The craft swung just clear of the mine, only to be rammed by a tank-landing craft only a few yards away from it. The L.C.A. was holed below the water line and the sea swamped in fast through a hole too jagged to be bunged. The Royal Marine coxswain called for full speed ahead on both engines.

"Starboard engine burnt out," came the answer. At this precise moment another craft collided with the L.C.A., knocking it broadside-on to the beach.

Still struggling with the wheel, the coxswain righted it and drove it close into the shore.

"Come on, boys—OUT!"

The troops leapt into three feet of water and waded ashore.

Then, lightened, the craft swung round and struck a mine. Miraculously no one was killed. But now snipers' bullets came whining down from high points beyond the beach.

The British invasion was on. The aim: to take the area between Bayeux and Caen and the sea that day. In the Gold sector was the 30th British Corps.

Here the surf was too rough to launch the amphibious DD tanks, and the assault plan had been modified at the last moment. First they would send in the specialized armor of Crabs (flail tanks), Crocodiles (flamethrowing tanks), and AVREs (armored vehicles, Royal Engineers). The last were the "demolition demons." Exactly at 0725 the first groups of Monty's armor rolled ashore from its landing craft and at once started clearing a way through the mines for itself and the infantry to follow. Four minutes after H-Hour, at 0729, the infantry dashed determined down the ramps and on to beaches swept with snipers' bullets. Later the DDs would beach behind the infantry.

First ashore on the right flank of Gold were the Hampshires—aptly since the invasion had largely assembled around Portsmouth and other parts of that county. Coming ashore right by Le Hamel, they found that this was the one area which had escaped the effects of the air and sea barrage. As the men bore bravely up the beach they were pinned in their tracks by accurate sustained fire from mortar and machine guns.

But although the Allied attack had not been able to pierce the strong reinforced concrete of the Le Hamel guns on the seaward, the Germans did not succeed in their hope of wiping out any troops advancing up this beach. First, they had assumed wrongly that the invaders would land at high tide and so be nearer than they were; second, that the assault could not be supported by armor, as the strongpoints were protected on the sea side. In fact, the Allied troops were out of effective range of enemy guns on landing, and by the time they were in it, the specialized armor had flailed ashore and provided cover for the infantry to clear the way.

The first sight to meet the men's eyes as they dug in wherever they could or tried for the sea wall were three Crab tanks, their flails furiously beating the beach to explode a way through the murderous mines. Defying all attempts to stop them, the Crabs continued up the sand. They could not last long, however, and were hit by enemy fire and stopped. Some of the crews staggered out and joined the infantry. One Crab actually got off the beach area and engaged an enemy strongpoint in a sanatorium overlooking the shore. But finally this Crab, too, went the way of the others.

Now the Dorsets dashed in beside the Hampshires at the next assault point, where the AVREs and other armored vehicles were more than a match for a sketchy defense system. They leveled practically every obstruction in sight; made sure that the patches of clay on the beach were well covered so that the DD tanks and others would not get stuck; filled in holes caused by shells from Allied or enemy fire; and erupted routes through the eternal mines. Then the Crabs really took the offensive, and within a couple of hours were bursting behind Arromanches to the westward.

In the Gold sector, as elsewhere throughout the British beachheads, well-laid plans were enforced to tackle the layer after layer of underwater and surface obstacles known to have been strengthened during the spring. In fact the Germans' western wall stretched right out to the tidal limits in such a way that they were covered at high tide. In fact, one of the reasons Montgomery landed at half tide was to make the job of tackling these submerged snares a little less hazardous. But the full advantage was not quite gained since, as has been mentioned, the tempestuous tide of that night and next morning swept the sea in thirty minutes or more ahead of its tabled time.

All along the beaches frogmen went in with the first fighting troops. They were men of the Royal Navy and Royal Marines like Lieutenant R. E. Billington, R.N.V.R., who commanded the courageous band of three other R.N.V.R. officers, a captain and five other noncommissioned Marines who led the Locker parties, Landing Craft Obstruction Clearance Units. Almost all had been engineers, carpenters and clerks before the war.

As their landing craft neared the shores from Arromanches to Ouistreham, they prepared for this operation which would have so vital an effect on later waves of craft. And they paid special attention to Element C. . . . These had been produced in considerable quantity and formed a formidable network designed to destroy any craft that hit them.

Element C was a 2½-ton mass of steel mesh, a 10-foot-high and 10-foot-broad picket fence under the water. Each one would have to be separately destroyed, as it could not be liquidated merely by a single explosion. But because the tide was running in early, more of each obstruction was covered than planned, and the frogmen looked apprehensively as they watched the water rolling inshore ahead of the landing craft. In addition they had to contend with hedgehogs, other steel obstacles looking like six-pointed stars,

160

and pyramids of metal objects standing some 5 feet high which were completely hidden by the tide.

Each of the vicious obstacles was festooned with mines or shells, so that the slightest touch by the bottom of a craft would let off a concentrated charge right below it. And even if a mine or shell failed to explode, it could tear a fatal hole in the light landing craft. These, then, were the enemies the frogmen had been training to tackle since January, for five intensive months, at H.M.S. Appledore on the secluded north Devon coast.

Coming in with the Green Howards and East Yorkshires on that east end of Gold beach opposite La Rivière, Lieutenant H. Hargreaves tried to remember everything he had learned at Appledore. Yet somehow it all seemed utterly strange. And as the craft came in close, German shells began to splutter in the surrounding water.

With Hargreaves were the eleven men in this unit. They were dropped into their small craft from a landing ship infantry at 0700. Hargreaves himself has said that many of them did not expect to return, yet were determined to carry out the work until it was completed.

The craft headed hell-for-leather toward the beach, hoping to find the front row of obstacles on the water's edge, but actually discovering them awash in three feet of sea. Hargreaves and another officer had the sector opposite La Rivière and slipped over the side of the craft before it beached. Trying to ignore the danger from enemy fire, they got to work on a row of posts with mines attached to the top of them.

They must have been still about four hundred yards from the beach when the first firing started. And there was nothing either of them could do about it save to try and forget it. So it was just as well that the job in hand took all their energies and attention. The double danger continued minute after minute that morning: the mines on top of the posts, and the chance of being hit by German bullets while half-hidden in the incoming tide.

After the posts Hargreaves had to face specially constructed wooden ramps, also mined, followed by steel hedgehogs complete with anti-aircraft shells and mines. As calmly as they could they

161

worked toward the shore, while shells, rockets, and even bombs fell all around them. It was a terribly exhausting task, but soon they had cleared an initial gap for the landing craft to use safely, and then they set to work to widen it as quickly as they could.

Their special kapok jackets, so long tested back in England, now proved able to protect them against the blast of mines and shells underwater. The trials in Horsea Lake had not been wasted. In fact the jacket saved the lives of three of Hargreaves' party a little further along the coast. Working just out of his depth in six feet of water, a naval petty officer frogman was suddenly stunned by a shell or mortar bomb exploding quite close. The blast knocked him unconscious, but one of his colleagues managed to swim over to him and help him to the surface. He was paralyzed by the shock for several hours but later recovered completely with no aftereffects at all. Without the jacket, he would never have survived the initial blast, for a Royal Engineer swimming toward the beach from an early-hit landing craft was killed outright by a similar explosion.

Another frogman dived for his first live mine obstruction and, groping around the base of a steel pole, found it. No sun shone through the murky water and the mine was attached so close to the bottom that the mud was churned up as he gripped it gently. For a second he held his breath behind his breathing equipment and then tried to relax. He could scarcely see the mechanism but somehow his fingers closed around the right part and in a few moments it was harmless. Half the job done. Then he set the small explosive charge to get rid of the obstruction itself, and as he swam to a safe distance it detonated bringing the pole toppling toward him. Not so bad as it might have been, he thought as he headed on to the next.

Meanwhile Hargreaves was finding it hard going purely from the physical angle. The heavy surf swept in powerfully toward the flat beach and he had difficulty keeping still enough to handle the endless mines and booby traps springing out all over the obstacles.

Slowly, however, he and the other frogmen forced their way in, until near the beach they were exposed to the added danger of sniping by the concealed Germans still within range of the shore in houses or elsewhere. Occasional stutters from machine guns raked the beach, too. This must have been worst of all: to be handling death in the water every minute and know that somewhere at their back snipers' guns were trained toward them.

On and on. There seemed no end to the obstacles. But Hargreaves and the others systematically destroyed them and eventually cleared a thousand yards of beach to a depth of four hundred yards. Altogether this party destroyed or disposed of 2,500 obstacles—practically every one of them mined.

Then "as a sort of savory," in Hargreaves' words, they cleared the explosives out of half a dozen beetle tanks and helped to winch drowning vehicles out of the water.

Hargreaves himself was wounded in the shoulder, but carried on with his job to win the Distinguished Service Cross. Then there was Marine Sergeant K. Briggs, who, single-handed, crouched in an exposed part of the beach and rendered a hundred charges safe—while being sniped at all the time.

The landings that gray morning cost two frogmen killed and ten wounded, some seriously. Ten per cent casualties—far less than expected for such an unpredictable job.

So the work went on, as landing craft of every kind poured through the gaps. Of course they could not clear more than an initial lane through the murderous mesh—there were far too few frogmen to do more. But nonetheless most of the craft came in safely. Many had to risk uncleared approaches, because the time element was vital and there was just no room for them all through the narrow safe channels.

Regularly after 0730 came rending sounds as landing crafts' bottoms scraped to a standstill against the obstacles and the men had to pile out into the water and swim ashore with full loads. Or if they were less lucky the obstacles ripped the bottoms right out of the boats, which were left in anything from two to ten feet of water. A few set off mines and sent spray spurting over the craft as they cracked with the blast. One moment men were crouched in an L.C.A., the next they struggled in the water. Yet not many were lost.

And all the time the frogmen worked: disconnecting the mines

163

in the gloom on the sea bed, then breaking up the obstructions of steel and concrete with their own explosives. But it was Element C which, in ten or more feet of water, was the ultimate nightmare. Totally submerged, the frogmen swam like ghosts, their arms stretched straight at the sides, around this strange, sinister steel-work. They planted 36 small charges one by one at strategic points of each structure, then swam out of the way as they exploded in a series of liquid pops. Only then did the entire structure fall quietly to pieces and lie safely on the bottom.

The craft came in through the gaps and ground to a halt. In the last yard or two, one of the big landing craft struck a Teller mine and death came to many of the men. Now other Tellers were taking their toll of craft and men, but the assault did not waver.

Luckily German resistance was less effective at La Rivière than at Le Hamel, for here the bombardment had done its job better. Much of the tiny town was a mere mass of jagged brickwork as the infantry stepped ashore. And here too, since the DD tanks could not get in yet, support craft came close behind the men in an attempt to cover them during the hectic moments of landing. Firing actually only a few feet above the heads of their own men, these floating support weapons set about finishing off the defenses that survived after the barrage. Sergeants waved to their platoons to follow them as they splashed through the water and dashed for cover. But by a fluke, the East Yorks landed at a point which had been untouched by the earlier holocaust or by the fire from the support craft. The men tore toward the sea wall for their very lives under a rain of bullets and shells. One fell dead. A bullet bit into the leg of another as he ran. He stopped for a second, dropped flat, and crawled for the wall.

An 88-mm. gun began shelling the vehicles as they drove ashore. It got a couple of the vital AVREs. A flail tank churned its way through the last yards of shallows and was about to touch the shingle when an 88-mm. shell hit it. Thick smoke poured out of it, but troops behind took advantage of the cover to race diagonally ashore as the wind blew the smoke southeast.

Then the shells again.

"Get down and don't bunch!" yelled a corporal. Less chance of casualties.

But the strongpoint did not last long. Its guns had a limited angle of fire and another flail tank which sped in at a sharp angle smashed it forever from a range of under 100 yards.

They were off the beach now, and in the grassy dunes as the Germans fell back to fresh positions, began machine-gunning the dunes. The thin grasses waved as the bullets flew overhead. Now the Tommies moved into extended order as they stepped cautiously over the rubble of a brick wall. Then on toward the town and close-weapon fighting from shop to shop.

Beside the East Yorks, the Green Howards had the beach, west of La Rivière. But here snipers stopped them in their damp tracks as they dug in wherever they could. Until the AVREs could get ashore things were at a standstill as, from the shelter of a wall, the Germans mixed grenades with snipers' fire. Then the AVREs reached the upper beach and under covering fire from two of them the infantry stormed up to the wall and hit the German point on the once peaceful sea road. After brief sharp resistance, the sight of the demolition vehicles sent the Germans into quick retreat. The value of armor was beginning to be apparent all along the British line.

D Company of the Green Howards negotiated a mine field with minor losses only to find themselves confronted by stronger enemy resistance. Their objective was the important Mont Fleury battery, which had already been well pasted by both the R.A.F. and the navy.

Despite resistance they were making good headway toward the battery when the company commander noticed that two of the enemy pillboxes on the route had been by-passed by the leading platoons. Thus began an action which earned the one Victoria Cross given as a result of D-Day.

Taking Company Sergeant Major Stanley Hollis with him, the commander went in to try and clear the pillboxes. But when they were only twenty yards from this live pillbox, a machine gun opened fire on them from the slit. C.S.M. Hollis instantly rushed straight at it, firing his Sten gun through the grid. A split second later Hollis jumped on top of the actual pillbox as he reloaded his weapon, forcing the small black magazine home. At the same time he wrenched out a grenade and threw it through the door of the pillbox, following it with more Sten fire. Two Germans dropped dead and Hollis rushed in and took the rest prisoner. Then as soon as they were safely taken, he ran over to a neighboring trench and cleared several Germans from it. By this action he certainly saved the rest of his company from heavy casualties from the rear, and thus enabled them to open the main beach exit from this end of Gold sector.

Taking the V.C. story on to its end, later on D-Day in the village of Crepon, the company encountered a field gun and crew armed with Spandaus. They were only a hundred yards away when Hollis was put in command of a party to cover an attack on the gun. Unfortunately the attack soon came under fire and was held up. Seeing this, Hollis pushed forward to engage the gun with a Piat from a house fifty yards away. He was observed by a German sniper, who fired and grazed his cheek. At the same second, the enemy gun swung round and fired into the house at point-blank range. Masonry started to fall all around them, so Hollis moved his party to another position. By this time two of the enemy gun crew had been killed, and the gun itself was destroyed soon afterward.

But then Hollis learned that two of his men had stayed behind in the house. He at once went to try and get them out. In full view of the enemy, and under constant fire, he went forward alone, using a Bren gun to distract the Germans' attention from his two men who, under cover of this heroic diversion, were able to scamper back to the company. Hollis, too, got back safely.

Wherever the fighting was heaviest throughout the day, Hollis displayed daring and gallantry, and on both these occasions he single-handedly prevented the enemy from stalling the advance of the Green Howards at critical stages.

As his citation concludes: It was largely through his heroism and resource that the company's objectives were gained and casualties were not heavier, by his own bravery he saved the lives of many of his men.

166

As C.S.M. Hollis was busy clearing the pillbox near the Mont Fleury battery, the reserve companies of the Green Howards came under mortar fire. C Company's commander was killed at once.

As Lieutenant Colonel Hastings' craft beached, their view was hidden by smoke. They passed the first obstacles—old rusty shells on poles sticking out of the water, as an AVRE on the beach exploded in a searing sheet of flame.

Hastings pointed to the spot where he wanted to land, but the L.C.M. was not responsive and they swung broadside on to the shore, missing the shells on poles by only a few feet. Then they came to premature rest a long way from the beach. Seeing the vessel was definitely grounded, Hastings called out:

"Lower ramps."

But nothing happened. The mechanism was broken. Then a huge ex-Guardsman put his square shoulder to it—and it opened. The beach looked far off and the water deep. Hastings walked to the edge of the ramp, sat down and dangled his feet over the edge— "not a very inspiring performance," he recalls. The water was only up to his knees! Without any difficulty they waded ashore and scrambled up the beach.

An occasional cry from within the wire of the mine field proved it was not a dummy lay. But as they reached the top of the incline, the first flail tank overtook them, having cleared a gap from the beach for vehicles. The operation was proceeding exactly to plan. Hastings ordered his tanks to follow up through this gap and they had completed the first phase of their duty. As he toured the companies he saw the mass of shipping still nosing inshore, and coming under mortar fire on the beach. But despite the enemy opposition still to be encountered, the most serious moment of the day for the 6th Battalion, the Green Howards, came when a friendly Frenchwoman plied them with cider so strong that their entire advance appeared to be endangered by drunkenness!

While the 30th British Corps hammered in on Gold beach, the 1st British Corps were landing in Juno and Sword sectors, the 3rd Canadian Division on Juno and the 3rd British on Sword. And away on the far left the 6th British Airborne Division was beyond the Orne. Due south of the line between Juno and Sword stood the prize that held the key to the whole ultimate success of the beachheads being bloodily established in these forenoon hours. Caen!

Reefs and rocks were added hazards in the central Juno sector and because of these and the tide the landings here had to begin later than on any other beach. The defenses thus received longest advance warning of the Allied approach. And even heading in as carefully as possible, several craft fouled on the rocks or went aground on the reefs, leaving them perfect targets.

Both the British sectors had stiff tasks, since the enemy's German mobile positions were known to be much stronger here than behind the Americans' coast. And here once again the weather prevented the amphibious tanks swimming ashore as planned so that they had to be discharged direct onto the beach later as at Gold beach.

Meanwhile, although H-Hour was fixed for 0735-0745, it soon was obvious the landings would be late as the Canadians' craft rolled uneasily through seas heavier even than elsewhere. Again the air and sea barrage missed most of the shore strongpoints and the stage seemed tragically set for a repetition of the raw savage slaughter already occurring on Omaha beach.

The tide was driving in violently now, washing above the middle of the underwater obstacles. The 0735 landing plan accepted as inevitable the fact that many obstacles would be submerged, but by now the situation was far worse. And each passing minute meant that the defenses had longer to revive from the noisy if inaccurate bombardment.

Yet most of the landing craft got through the maze of mined obstacles at the low-water mark. To the usual near-misses and occasional hits, they hit the beaches about Courseulles-sur-Mer around 0800. At this late hour, the engineers had little time to tackle the obstructions before the tide made it a task for frogmen.

The troops of the 7th Canadian Brigade picked a way ashore actually through the beach booby traps, to be greeted with a withering fire from both sides of the mouth of the Seulles. They looked around for the AVREs or some armor—but none was in sight. The assault vehicles were well back because of the difficulty of plowing a path through the surf. Then with a debacle threatening, the Canadian infantry whistled with relief as they saw the first batch of DD tanks. The tank-landing craft had come in to half a mile from high-water mark and dropped them among the mines. One or two at once had their floats or tracks blasted by mines, but the rest came roaring out of the shallows to support the men.

The troops rushed the beach with dramatic daring, pouring Sten gunfire into the pillboxes and foxholes while the DDs loosed their heavy arms at the largest fortifications. Buoyed by their success, the infantry pushed inland at a mile an hour, only to have the inevitable crowding of vehicles and armor on the beach slow up the second wave of the assault. Nevertheless by 1000, only two hours after touch down, all beach objectives had been gained: great credit to these tough Canadians who had been training all spring in the rugged uplands of Surrey.

But while the Canadians stormed the beach, the tide rose still further and now the empty landing craft returning to sea ran into trouble with the outer rows of obstacles. Of one battalion's 24 landing craft, all except four failed to get back to their parent ships, either being sunk by mines or rent against the steelwork.

The 8th Canadian Brigade attacked opposite Bernières quite alone. This was a narrow front and the sea swirled angrily around the rocks. To try and launch the tanks through the surf would be bound to fail. So it was up to the troops. Canadians and French-Canadians.

The early craft came reeling in on top of the surf and were deposited higher than expected on the beach. As they suddenly found themselves there, with the waves receding, they discovered a stretch of only a hundred yards separated them from the sea wall at the back of the beach.

But every yard of it was covered and cross-covered by the weapons of the Bernières defenders.

One company sprinted straight for the wall. Half of them never reached it. Some only got a few yards, then fell, to lie still as the incoming tide lapped about them.

Yet in less than a quarter of an hour, the Canadian first troops took all the strongpoints, the last one falling when a flak ship ran the gauntlet of rocks and guns to land opposite the enemy and blast them from a range of the width of the beach. The follow-up regiment landing soon after 0800 met only sniping. Then the armor came ashore, with the troops supporting it instead of the other way round. And as it engaged the few Germans remaining, the infantry swept into Bernières. French-Canadians liberating the land of their forefathers.

Apart from the infantry, the worst losses here were to major landing craft bringing in the armor as beach obstacles and Teller mines took their toll.

What was it really like? Here's one Canadian's reactions. Cliff Bowering was there with them.

"That dryness in your mouth, the tongue like cotton wool, the cold, unreasoning slab in your belly. The sense of anticipation that defies description.

"Your heartbeat trying to outdo the sound of gunfire and bombs. The wondering of what it will be like on the beach.

"All the old clichés running through your head. Your nervous smile—but the effort hurts your dried lips.

"Somebody laughs, only it sounded more like a croak. And it was too loud. The one-in-every crowd wise guy. . . .

" 'Home was never like this . . . not much like the old ferry back home . . . I wonder who's missing me now . . . it's Paris first chance I get . . . anyone for tennis. . . .'

" 'Can the chatter back there, we're going in.'

"The exact minute had arrived.

"The ramp crashes down. You see what looks like ten miles of water between you and the beach. For the first time you realize two things . . . somebody's shooting at you and there are a hell of a lot of ships on either side. And you're shooting back with a barrage that stuns the imagination.

"You're in the water now. In the breakers. You try to remember how to walk in the water and keep your rifle up and dry. Yard by yard you move in. Smoke up ahead and the noise . . . it's like nothing you've ever heard before, even in the blitz. What a difference between this and battle camp. Brother, this is for real!

"Wade some more. Shells sloughing into the water near a barge. *Chug-crunch.* A barge hit. A man goes down and you lunge forward in fear. But he's up again—only stumbled. Beach up ahead. Another man down. He doesn't get up. Tracer to the left. Machine guns. Planes diving in—R.A.F. You lovely babies from hell!

"In the background the steady rumble and swoosh of the navy guns. God bless 'em! Softening up, they called it. And all last night and this morning pounding, pounding, pounding the pride of the Third Reich.

"Your head tucked into your shoulders like a boxer weaving toward his target. Smaller target that way? Crouching lower as you walk, pretending you can't be seen—maybe.

"Your mouth dryer still. Hoping you don't have to speak, because you couldn't. Rifle up higher. You're on the beach. Rifle at the port. Shells coming in on the right. Machine guns. Men falling. Funny, no one around you has been hit. This isn't so bad after all.

"You think pretty clearly after that. Now you know what all that training was for. This is the job and things are going well. Too easy . . . a dull smack, a groan. The man beside you goes down, doesn't move. Face in the water. You move on. Sniper? Sniper, hell! That's a machine gun. Let's go. Up to the sea wall and down and wait for orders. Orders.

"The tanks didn't get in ahead of you like they planned. One of those things. You move on. Town called Bernières. One company badly shot up. Not yours, thank God."

Soon he was in Courseulles, and the Canadian who had cracked about Paris could at least claim to have taken over the Hôtel de Paris there, off causeway No. 6, which was henceforth *Interdit aux Civiles*.

Next came the Commandos.

Sixteen

A SALUTE is due the Royal Marines. Ten thousand took part in the D-Day operation. Two-thirds of the assault landing craft delivering the infantry on the beaches were manned by Marines. Through the stormy seas, they brought the fleet safely to landfall, and even then their job was not always done. Take the case of Sergeant Cecil Hunter.

Just before reaching one of the Juno beaches, his L.C.A. took a damaging hit. The troops piled out, but the marine crew could not return as planned. Sergeant Hunter and his crew had to take to the beach, where he at once looked around to see what he could do to help in the assault. Nearby, the Canadians were exchanging fire with German mortars and snipers, and trying to keep in contact with the captain of a tank beached thirty yards away.

Hunter immediately appointed himself messenger between the Canadian sergeant major and the tank captain who had to communicate if some sort of plan were to be made to get off that beach. Only thirty yards intervened—but the beach was constantly swept with fire from rifles, mortars, and other heavier guns. Across this death trap Hunter crawled to take the first message. He waited while an answer was made, then returned to deliver the reply. Snipers saw him and concentrated their fire on him so that he had some close shaves before getting back to comparative cover. Then the fight flared again, and once more he had to crawl across those open yards. Every move could have been his last. Then he crawled back with another answer, making four journeys in all. Somehow he survived to win the Conspicuous Gallantry Medal.

And then there were the Royal Marine Commandos. Five formations went into action on D-Day, the first two—48 and 41—linking the Juno and Sword sectors. 48 Commando was to land next to the Canadians and swing left, while 41 was to land beside the British on Sword and swing right.

As had happened elsewhere, the preliminary bombardment left the defenses at St. Aubin-sur-Mer almost unscathed, as the marines' six little landing craft jogged inward. Two of them were jolted more than merely by the sea, however, as they suddenly struck obstacles in quick succession, and both began to sink at once, quite a way still from shore. Quickly the Commandos jumped clear of the craft and tried to swim ashore, only to have the tidal stream sweep many of them away to be drowned beneath the weight of water and equipment. Some staggered into their depths, though, behind the other craft.

The moment they beached, the Commandos met heavy machine-gun, mortar and shell fire. Colonel Moulton, the commanding officer, almost immediately took a splattering of splinters as a mortar bomb burst near him. Dazed, he dashed on. Captain Reynolds, leading the vanguard troop, ran into intense machine-gun fire right on the beach and had both his arms broken. Still he carried on till he reached cover.

Wounded were dotted all over the beach now and the padre, Rev. J. Armstrong, R.N., stayed there exposed tending and comforting them as best he could until he was hit and badly wounded himself. This was the church in action. Here was the word of God.

Then the survivors of the wrecked landing craft came ashore into this inferno and one was killed at once. But before long the Commandos reached their assembly area, where a quick count showed a strength of 70 per cent. Captain Reynolds insisted upon carrying on, sitting smoking cigarettes lit for him by one of his troop, until the beach eventually was cleared and he was ordered evacuated with the other wounded.

Depleted but undaunted, the Commandos grouped themselves ready for their task of taking the German strongpoint at Langrune about a thousand yards inland, with its formidable collection of mines, trenches and pillboxes.

Meanwhile, four miles farther east, just into the Sword Sector, 41 Troop under Lieutenant Colonel Gray encountered even worse difficulties. Its two objectives were to destroy the German strongpoint known to exist at Lion-sur-Mer, and to assault a suspected one in a château inland. Accordingly the troop was to be divided into two forces on landing. Through no fault of Gray, the plan went wrong at once. Half an hour before beaching, he had received a signal saying that the beach would not be under fire, yet as they touched down, fierce fire greeted the men and caused havoc: Major Barclay who was to have led the château force was killed, and Captains Stratford and Morris were wounded. So Gray took over the château force himself, and immediately had to halve it to send help to the Lion-sur-Mer force facing the German strongpoint. And since both their radio sets had been damaged on the landing beach, they could not summon any support fire from the navy. Desperate fighting went on all during the morning while they gradually got to a group of houses near the strongpoint. Later in the day, both 48 and 41 Troops achieved their objectives, but until they did the success of the advance of the 3rd British Division off Sword revolved on the ability of the Commandos to neutralize the Lion-sur-Mer strongpoint. And the 3rd Division was the cornerstone to Operation Overlord.

H.M.S. *Arethusa* and the rest of the warships in Naval Force S laid down by far the most effective bombardment of any along the coast that morning on to the Sword strip between Lion-sur-Mer and Ouistreham, a distance of three miles. First, the smoke and flashes from heavy guns against the lead-gray horizon; then the flashes ashore as the shells straddled the 800-yard-deep strip of shore under attack. From 0515 to 0715 the attack roared, and in the middle of it, Fortresses and Liberators released a rain that made the ground shake and shudder. Once more the fighter bombers swept in almost at sea level, just high enough to be above the naval guns. And then came a heartening sight: a French squadron with the Cross of Lorraine painted poignantly on their sides. From their hard-won positions inland on the Orne, the airborne troops listened to the bombing and looked over the few intervening miles as each fresh eruption lit up the dawn in startling silhouette.

Nought seven fifteen: A crashing crescendo—then sudden silence as the landing craft covered the few remaining yards to Sword beach.

But out at sea, unheard above the bombardment, a drama was taking place. Despite a fairly heavy sea, two squadrons of DDs started to swim ashore from 4,500 yards. These were overtaken by L.C.T.s with AVREs. All went well for a mile or so, with German opposition restricted to shellfire from light batteries ashore, the accuracy of which was hampered by bad visibility so that losses were negligible. But then a flotilla of large L.C.T.s headed in right before the bows of the amphibious tanks. In a moment, two of the tanks—scarcely suited at best to navigate in a sea like this—had been hit by the tank-landing craft and sunk. Luckily, a group of enemy rockets spluttering in the sea all around the L.C.T.s forced them to adjust course. No more tanks were rammed and by splendid navigation, the crews of the amphibians managed to avoid further accident.

Captain Denny's tank was 700 yards from the beach when it sank after this collision. He was thrown clear and picked up half an hour later, but although the rest of the crew had Mae Wests and escape apparatus they never appeared again. All the crew of the other sunk tank were saved.

Nought seven twenty-five: about half of the tanks reached Queen beach in the Sword sector abreast of the infantry. They touched down well to seaward of the beach obstacles and moved forward to deflate, so that they could run on land. Then, hulls down in the water, they set about trying to neutralize enemy fire from houses and emplacements. Some tanks were inevitably knocked out by shellfire, while others were swamped in the shallows by breakers. Despite flooded turrets, these tanks kept firing until the guns were awash and the crew had to bale out and cover the rest of the 200 to 300 yards to the beach in their rubber dinghies, highly exposed to the enemy.

Other armor arrived actually just ahead of the first waves of DD tanks, so that as the L.C.A.s beached between 0725 (H-Hour here) and 0730, they already had the support of tanks and clearance vehicles as planned.

As the assault started, the midget subs' job ended, and X.20 off Arromanches, and X.23 just a little way out off the Orne, headed north again. Soon they would be back in Blockhouse sleeping soundly.

But not the South Lancs or East Yorks. Exactly at 0730, as the armor opened fire from the water's edge, the South Lancs slid ashore and cleared their craft safely and swiftly. The defense seemed slightly less strong here than at other points, perhaps because of the British supporting armor.

But even so, the troops walked into a stutter of Spandaus and through the inevitable haze of smoke. Mortars coughed and shells fell among the men until the DDs cracked into action again and the enemy fire slackened.

C Squadron of wading Sherman tanks followed ashore at 0810, which was just as well since the first two squadrons were badly depleted by now. Out of the twenty tanks in A Squadron, only six survived, yet their job was done well. And when the lead tank of B Squadron moved up the beach, only one other tank of the squadron's twenty was in sight. These two joined forces and reached the sand dunes. Unable to cross them, Captain Neave brought a bulldozer up to force a gap through and soon the shore was more or less clear and the South Lancs were rapidly prodding forward into the dunelands.

By 0830 the infantry and the AVREs flailing away up the beach had cleared a couple of exits for the tanks left, and within the next hour they swung rapidly right to reach Hermanville.

C Squadron now blew off its special waterproofing and moved toward these newly made beach exits, leaving the beach still congested with men and vehicles.

Meanwhile our little group of Warwickshires had stumbled ashore toward their gabled-end house, which by now seemed as familiar as the residence of an old relation. Guiding them safely ashore, it beckoned them up the beach to cover. No one seemed hurt, thanks to their mascot, the house. Now it had played its part, and they hastened on to their real objective, which ironically was—the cemetery!

Then they met their first Frenchman, complete with shabby beret, spectacles and an F.F.I. armband. "Mine, mine!" he shouted, pointing to their intended route across the fields. Nevertheless they plowed on, mine detectors to the fore, and no mine revealed itself. Soon they reached the cemetery and dug in.

They enjoyed ten minutes of peace before snipers, rifles and machine guns began to be heard.

"We're in the right spot," someone whispered grimly.

Their own sniper team went stalking silently through the nearby corn to track the German snipers, and soon one of them tumbled from a tree. One of the Warwickshires was hit in the knee and had to limp back to base. Then they cleared out of the cemetery and pressed on—leaving about a dozen men crumpled there. . . .

Farther east at Ouistreham, the landing craft bearing the East Yorks drove relentlessly through barricades of beach obstacles to get ashore. Here the opposition was stronger than on adjacent beaches and they had to fight their way from one position to the next. Once more the Commandos came to the rescue and helped rid the east end of the beach of small-arms fire.

The 45 Troop Commandos under Lieutenant Colonel Ries forming part of Brigadier Lord Lovat's 1st Special Service Brigade landed safely on the western outskirts of Ouistreham. After covering the beach for the East Yorks, they proceeded to their main task of crossing the Caen Canal and the River Orne, and seizing a bridgehead on the far side of the river, thus securing the left flank of the whole Allied perimeter. They carried rubber dinghies and collapsible bicycles with them but the dinghies were not needed, since the 6th Airborne Division had carried out its attack from the east of the Orne so well that the Germans had been so surprised they had neglected to blow up the bridges.

Ries led his men across the intact bridges, but a sniper got the colonel in his sights and he had to retire wounded. Major Gray took over from him and 45 Commando pushed steadily north toward Merville, which they knew to be already in the hands of the Allied airborne troops. So the beaches began to take shape, but at 1000 hours on D-Day it was still too early to claim complete success.

Seventeen

You could call it a beachhead—just. As the second wave of assault troops swarmed ashore on beaches from Utah to Sword, the battle began in ruthless reality: the fight for a foothold. Craft carrying the initial wave of assault troops returned north and crossed the path of the next wave. This time along with the troops came jeeps, tanks, guns.

Still the sea proved an implacable enemy. The tide was higher now and many of the landing craft could not get far enough inshore. As they lowered their ramps, the waves either tilted them to an impossible angle or caused them to snap off altogether as if broken by some angry giant. So the men were left either to jump for it, into three, four or five feet of water, or slide desperately down the buckled ramps. And ashore it was still the same story as before on many of the beaches. Shells, bombs, bodies.

Utah was no worse nor better than most. The special squads were still struggling against the mines and obstacles with inadequate equipment. And now they came under steady shelling. Too often the way through the mines was marked only by a wounded engineer waiting to be evacuated. But by 1000 hours they had cleared minimum gaps for the reinforcement regiment to land. Ignoring the shells, the fresh troops moved northwest toward the area intended for the first landings.

Jeeps, tanks and guns all came flooding ashore, marking the signal for the infantry to strike out across the causeways over the flooded regions just behind the beaches. The amphibious tanks actually moved through these flooded areas, leaving the causeways for the infantry. There was only spasmodic shelling now

181

as the Germans dropped back before the armor. Then at noon came the first link-up between the forces from the sea and those dropped by air. At the far end of the causeways the Americans met their airborne comrades who had been charged with seizing the exits from the causeways. In places, the Americans had penetrated up to 10,000 yards inland. In view of what was happening over at Omaha, this was reassuring news to receive.

For as German shells still dropped on Omaha, the only thing for the men to do was to dig down into the soft sand so that only a direct hit would get them. So behind the cover of jeeps or trucks, they burrowed down, while the engineers struggled to get to grips with the hidden yet ever-present mines.

Nought nine thirty: not only had the Americans lost men and materials, they were disorganized and still pinned down along the beach by intense enemy fire.

At 1000 a message went out from beach headquarters: "There are too many vehicles on the beach; send combat troops. Thirty L.C.T.s waiting offshore; cannot come in because of shelling. Troops dug in on beaches, still under heavy fire."

As soon as the commander received this signal he dispatched the next assault wave and moved destroyers in almost to the beach to blast the German positions. Although the Americans were dug in perilously near the enemy posts, the ships sent salvo after salvo whistling just over them at the Germans, and this helped to break the deadlock. To the men still on the beach, it seemed a long six hours since 0630. All that had happened before D-Day was like another age. Their lives had begun at dawn and already some had ended.

The destroyers stopped engines now, a mere half mile offshore, and as they traded fire with the coastal guns the American assault troops landed in knee-deep water. More engineers came in too, their tools strapped to their backs. And to cover the second landings came the rest of the amphibious tanks, brought right in to shore by ship.

The troops needed every vehicle and weapon that could be mustered, but still the vital thing was to widen the narrow paths through the mine fields. Tanks could not yet pass and vehicles were still accumulating. All through that long, seemingly endless morning the GIs battled to get the hell off that bloody beach.

High tide came and forced the vehicles to crowd still closer together. M.P.s arrived to try the impossible and bring order out of this chaos. And despite the destroyers, shells still fell steadily onto the Omaha stretch as the second wave beached and emerged from their landing craft into a flashing furnace of smoke, death and destruction. Now they were about ready to burst out of those shell- and hell-swept shores. Slowly they began to get off Easy and Fox beaches.

So the order was to get off the beaches and up the bluffs. Heading from west to east for Vierville, St. Laurent, Colleville.

Still the men seemed to think of themselves as being "mentally pinned down" behind the sea wall, but gradually six hundred men struggled off Dog White, just east of Vierville. Bunching near the edge of the bluffs did not help hurry matters, but scattered formations did reach the village during mid-morning, depite fire from machine guns in the hedgerows which hindered them spasmodically.

Vierville fell about 1100 hours and detachments of Rangers and the 116th Infantry passed through it before noon, only to be again halted by fire from hedgerows which ran at right angles to the highway. Each time they tried to advance, enemy rifles and automatics spat fire from a range of only two or three hundred yards. At last the decision was made to call off the advance along the coastal road and concentrate elsewhere.

Sniped at all the way, the command group of the 116th also reached Vierville by noon, and small skirmishes went on all around the area, with some fifteen Germans being killed. Much later, Colonel Canham found out for the first time what had happened on the beaches in front of Vierville. This flank remained the weakest all throughout the day, with exits from the beaches only beginning to be found by dark.

Back on those beaches, at 1300, heavy naval guns including the main batteries of the *Texas* directed their attention to guarding the Dog areas. The destroyer *McCook* radioed ashore that through their glasses they could see Germans leaving emplacements to surrender. Thirty prisoners were quickly grabbed.

As soon as the barrage lifted, General Cota set out for the beach to see why no traffic was getting through inland. Accompanied by only four men, he crept all the way down, past the strongpoints and the antitank wall, and out once more on to the flat fearful beach—without drawing more than scattered small-arms fire. Five Germans, taken prisoner from holes in the cliffside, led them through a mine field on the way.

The 121st Engineer Combat Battalion, responsible for clearing the main Dog exit, had lost three-quarters of its gear on landing and suffered heavy casualties, too. Precious time was lost in collecting men and salvaging equipment, a task performed to the accompaniment of snipers' fire from a dozen strongpoints. Meanwhile cleaning out the enemy became difficult in the Hamel au Prêtre region, where their fortifications were linked by long tunnels.

Fourteen thirty: Lieutenant Charles Parker and his men left the château he had taken south of Vierville to head for the 5th Rangers assembly area, by Pointe du Hoe. Preceded by a dozen prisoners, they got as far as some prepared German position before being stopped. They tried to bull through, but found themselves outflanked and all but surrounded; to extricate themselves they left the roads and struck out across country.

Now back to Easy and the St. Laurent zone. Certainly anything less aptly named than Easy could scarcely be conceived. At 1000, M Company was still pinned to the beach, while the 3rd Battalion of the 116th was only beginning to stagger up to the high ground. The total distance to be gained during the day around St. Laurent was only half a mile. A mere 800-odd yards. But from 1000 till noon there was little progress, only skirmishes and stiffening resistance. A company of Germans controlling the approaches to the main crossroad, and with good fields of fire, caught a small American group by surprise machine-gun fire. The rest of the 2nd Battalion remained pinned at the same crossroad all afternoon.

The 115th Infantry landing on Easy Red at high noon took

184

most of the afternoon to clear the beach, and St. Laurent held them up further. As their transport was not due in on D-Day, the men had to carry heavy loads, which did not help them in combat. In addition, the 2nd Battalion had to cope with fire from its own naval guns, whose shells were landing around them near the village. So elements of five battalions spent most of the day advancing across an area of one square mile, containing only pockets of resistance. The reason: lack of communications and control, and absence of artillery and armored support.

After reaching Vierville and St. Laurent by noon, the slowdown assumed an air of inevitability. The one vital battalion of artillery which got ashore during the whole day on those deathly Dog beaches encountered systematic shelling and mortar fire. It had set out for shore with a dozen guns. Some it lost on the rough run-in or on landing, others to enemy fire, until by the afternoon it had but one gun left.

By 0900 the original 16th Regiment got past the bluff and forced a thin wedge inland toward Colleville, moving a thousand yards south in an hour. Then followed a heavy house-to-house engagement on the outskirts of the town in which they were joined by small sections of the 116th. By a misunderstanding these sections then withdrew to a specified bivouac area, leaving the enemy to filter through the gaps thus left. Since a pillbox overlooking Fox Green beach had swiveled its guns round inland to the south, the 16th now found that they were in a three-sided vise—if not completely encircled. For several hectic hours, they fought a desperate defensive action which came closest to being an enemy counterattack as experienced at Omaha during the entire day.

With the situation becoming more serious each hour, a battalion of the 18th Infantry, the reinforcement regiment, swept up to relieve them and drove the Germans back in bitter fighting. Here at the western entrance to Colleville, the 16th struggled against a dramatic backdrop of scudding clouds, tall trees, ripped roofs, and the strangely stark silhouette of a wrecked church, its windows smashed and gaping.

All day this sense of isolation persisted, with little enemy groups materializing in areas supposed to be cleared. Advances became blind and coordination was out of the question. And with the isolation inevitably went a feeling of unreality. Am I really here fighting in Normandy on D-Day? Or is it all a dream—or nightmare?

The reinforcing 18th landed on Easy Red from 1100 to 1400, and General Wyman turned one company after another from their original missions to take over those of the 16th. As they advanced, the enemy fire proved to be ideally situated for covering strategic spots like gates and hedgerow openings. Typical of the fluid state of things was the experience of G Company of the original 16th, which found itself with little resistance ahead, but under fire from *behind*.

To the extreme east, the 3rd Battalion of the 16th, on its own since dawn, drove south toward Cabourg, but a three-man patrol ran right into the enemy and was captured. With Cabourg held in strength, no major advance was possible there, even with the welcome addition of seventeen tanks.

Afternoon on the beaches from Dog Green to Fox Red saw three miles and more of ordered confusion as spasmodic shelling from the navy reduced strongpoints, while German artillery inland returned the fire from the beaches. Easy Green got the worst of this, and even quite late direct shell hits sunk or fired several landing craft. Vehicles trying to escape the artillery began to move laterally along the beach, looking for safer exits than Les Moulins. Despite the steady stream of artillery fire, the American engineers determinedly forced their way through the obstacles. By now they were used to the flurry of bullets beating in the sand around them. But as the tide ebbed, the task eased a little, and by evening thirteen gaps were marked.

Meanwhile the landings went on according to plan—as far as time was concerned if not always in the right place. For example a signal said:

"Fox Beach ready for development."

So the 336th Battalion of engineers scheduled to land there headed for shore—only to beach at the other end of Omaha, 4,000 yards away!

At 1500 hours, an engineer unit had to cross Fox Green in the face of severe shelling. Moving silently in pairs, half the men had made it successfully, when a bulldozer working near the shingle took a direct hit and flamed into a molten mass. The only consolation was that the smoke covered the rest of the movement. Over at Fox Red, the 336th lost six men, but a trailer loaded with explosives and towed by a tractor negotiated the nerve-racking trip completely unscathed.

Under cover of fire from the sea, vehicles moved inland. Between 1200 and 1300, bulldozers cut a road up the western slope toward St. Laurent, despite the fact that they were under sniper fire. Preloaded DUKWs grounded on Easy Red and Green an hour later, with the Germans lacking artillery observation necessary for accurate firing on the vital exits. But by 1500 enemy resistance around St. Laurent caused another pause, as vehicles were jammed bumper to bumper all along the road. Once more the engineers came to the rescue by clearing a branch road.

Both the exhausted 16th and the comparatively fresh 18th awaited their armor. They had to hang on until well into the afternoon, as it was 1400 hours before the first tanks and other armored vehicles rumbled ashore and headed for the one available exit. And even then, the concentration of targets attracted sustained German shelling. One shell exploded right on a jeep, ripping it and its occupants to pieces.

These first few tanks meant that the infantry had a chance to hold the places they had won. Right round the clock the foot soldiers had been facing odds, thin columns of men on foot beating off the German pockets while the build-up on the beach proceeded painstakingly.

Back by the coast, the Allied naval barrage had stopped altogether now, since the ships did not know exactly where the Americans were advancing, and aircraft could not probe the confused lines, made even more confused by the screen of smoke suspended over most of Omaha.

So the German shells went on falling as support troops landed and the artillery finally rolled ashore. Gun carriers towing anti-tank guns splashed through the ebbing tide. Yet even now the unfortunate bad weather made matters difficult. The seas swamped

187

six howitzers being borne ashore on DUKWs. The other half dozen of the battalion, however, were tied in together and fired their first salvo at 1615, offering a warm teatime for the machine-gun nest near Colleville which was the target.

More heavy howitzers arrived now, from 1500 to 1830, but not without more losses. Five guns were rendered useless as their L.C.T.s met mishaps in the shallow waters. But guns got ashore safely, as losses rose to 26 guns, 25 vehicles, and a great deal of other gear. With the beachhead so narrow, medical units had been unable to set up stations yet, and treatment was in temporary quarters.

The sun was going down to the accompaniment of sniper fire and the occasional heavier thuds of exploding shells. A maze of debris littered the shingle on Dog beach, with discarded life preservers everywhere. Tangled barbed wire, wrecked LCA 1063, the tops of Element C, a stray barrage balloon and broken boxes of demolitions. Some GIs dug into a pillbox being used as temporary H.Q. on Easy Red.

No, it hadn't been easy, especially since the armor arrived only just in time to meet the threat of a Panzer counterattack. If the Germans had known it, an attack in force against Omaha that evening might have had a far-reaching influence. But they allowed the Allies gradually to land vital armor, and this was where the American flair for mechanization would rebound against them.

Now the GIs were a mile inland at Colleville. A few stray civilians waved encouragement to the advance units, standing before the hollow shells of their homes. Others who had homes looked out from their scarred shutters.

By evening the balance had definitely swung the way of the liberators. The American infantry, who had forced footholds in North Africa and last summer in Sicily, were not going to be beaten now. Still outgunned, they cut the Colleville-St. Laurent road and broadened their front to the four-mile width of the original landings. Even Colonel Taylor who had led them off the beach had not expected to see such a swing of the pendulum after those first three hours of hell.

Omaha at dusk was still under heavy enemy fire from mortars

and longer-range artillery. What had been achieved there during that day? The greater parts of five regiments were ashore, but as for equipment of every sort, only 100 tons of the 2,400 tons planned to reach the beaches arrived by the end of D-Day—an amazingly low proportion. Luckily, most of the 110 preloaded DUKWs landed, or else the ammunition would have run out entirely.

Casualties ran into several thousands, as well as over fifty tanks and much other equipment. And fifty landing craft and ten larger vessels never reached the Normandy shore on Omaha.

Even so, the situation might have been immeasurably worse with the presence of enemy aircraft. If German fighters or fighter-bombers could have intervened over Omaha in the critical early morning stage, anything might have happened. As it was, Allied air supremacy proved absolute. Only three Focke-Wulfe 190s appeared, to be rudely chased off by air patrols sweeping over the beaches.

Not until nightfall when 22 planes attacked shipping without causing serious damage did the Luftwaffe get anywhere near Omaha. One bomb did drop only 35 yards from the battleship *Arkansas,* but three aircraft were shot down during this attempted attack.

Over in England, Eisenhower and Montgomery had heard the reports coming in from the airborne and later the American and British beaches. As soon as they saw that the landings were fairly successful, Montgomery hurried off in a launch to board a destroyer on its way from Portsmouth to Normandy. Not only did he want to visit the beaches at the very earliest possible time, but he had to decide on the best place to set up his advanced headquarters. Now that the Allies were ashore he wanted to be on the spot. Eisenhower promised to visit him the following day, and naturally chose Omaha for his first call.

But now the second wave was ashore along Omaha—and with tanks, too. For the five thousand ships and craft used in the whole operation it was time to get back to base to take on further loads. For those which were not resting on the bottom or being broken

189

up by the tide as they lay a few feet above water level, that is. These would all have to be cleared away to make way for the following supply craft.

Meanwhile one L.S.T. disgorged its tanks on Omaha during the afternoon and headed north. Halfway across the Channel it encountered a German E-boat which sent a torpedo racing toward it. The tank-landing craft shuddered as it hit her amidships. Nearly severed in two by the explosion, her hull was held together only by a few rivets and strips of torn metal. But the sublieutenant commanding her refused to abandon hope. The Isle of Wight was almost in sight now. Slowing down to avoid as much strain as he could, he nursed her home into the Solent, the great rent in her hull seemingly gaping wider each moment.

Another craft took several German shells on her deck, then was broken clean in two by the weather. Undismayed and behaving as if this were a normal experience in the English Channel, the crew made both halves watertight and getting up steam in the after end, containing the engines, moved ahead of the severed fore end. Getting ropes across the water to the fore end, they then proceeded to head for home, which they reached safely—back to front!

Ten hundred: Gold beach. The frogmen and engineers fighting against time, the enemy, and the elements, were desperately clearing sea lanes through the maze of underwater obstacles, as the second wave assault forces were due to land. These follow-up brigades actually touched down an hour later to give everyone ashore extra time. And as the obstacles yielded to expert demolition and half a dozen exits from the beaches were established, the beach groups worked miracles of control so that there were hardly any traffic blocks.

Now men and munitions poured ashore. Men weighed down with 90 pounds of equipment waded off landing ships into water five feet deep. Clutching their precious ammunition boxes shoulder-high, they turned their backs on the battered ships with their white ensigns riddled but hanging proudly. Still a blazing bedlam, the beach presented a picture of chaos despite the now efficient traffic control. A wounded man lay on his stomach and waited, hoping for the best as the flash of a shell reflected gold in the studs of his soles and horseshoes of his heels. Near him, men still dug in as they waited for their turn to advance beside Churchill tanks with names painted gaily on their sides. Gun barrels pointed grimly inland, radio aerials ready for orders to move those thick treads.

But here at least the worst of the initial beach battle was over. After landing from 1100 onward, both reinforcement brigades had cleared the beaches in an hour or so, and the advance spearhead had reached two miles inland.

Afternoon now, and the Germans falling back before the methodical Montgomery strategy of infantry plus armor. Striking southwest the Tommies pushed six miles from Gold, cutting the Bayeux road and reaching the main Bayeux-Caen road. The two relief brigades made really spectacular advances, but as they did so, the original assault team of Green Howards and East Yorks had gotten just as far from the beaches, capping a tremendous twelve-hour effort. By sunset the 30th British Corps controlled some thirty square miles, and had its patrols on the perimeter of Bayeux and had occupied Creully.

Only on the extreme right did resistance continue throughout the afternoon from the German garrison at Le Hamel. It was this stubborn strongpoint which nearly wrecked the most ambitious operation of the R.M. Commandos during the entire invasion at the outset.

At the extreme western end of the British sector the little fishing harbor of Port-en-Bessin stood in a tiny hollow among an imposing line of chalk cliffs. These are the cliffs beginning in the Omaha sector. Rising to a height of two hundred feet, they have been deeply scarred by the inroads of sea and rain through the centuries.

Port-en-Bessin, while not exactly a major port, was situated so as to be a good supply center. Realizing its strategic value, the Germans had strengthened its defenses and in doing so had taken every advantage of the rugged surrounding terrain.

Lieutenant Colonel C. F. Phillips leading the 47 Commando

had orders to capture this little fortress lying between Gold and Omaha beaches: the pivotal point for the American and British link-up. For weeks beforehand, Phillips and his men had been training for this task in the hills of Dorset, but even so they could not know exactly how the actual assault would go. All that seemed certain was that the post must be impervious to a frontal assault, so that the only alternative was to attack from the rear.

Their plan began with a landing within the beachhead of the 30th British Corps. Once ashore at the right hand of Gold, they were to force a way westward and inland across eight to ten miles of enemy-held country until they were behind the port. They would have no vehicles in support, so all their weapons, ammunition and the explosives to demolish any enemy fortifications they encountered, had to be carried on their backs. The average weight of each man's pack amounted to 88 pounds.

The fourteen landing craft of 47 Commando headed for the beach where the Hampshires had just landed to find Le Hamel almost untouched by the dawn barrage. Shells from the coast began to fall closer to the craft as they neared the beach. To attempt a landing at the point intended would have meant disaster for a force whose one aim was to break out of the beach at once and travel far and fast. Thus they diverted their course east for a mile and a half.

Now they encountered their next setback. On the run into the beach between the twin assault of the Hants and Dorsets, four of their fourteen craft struck obstacles submerged only a few inches below the surface and the Teller mines attached literally blew the craft out of the water. Desperately the Commandos fought to free themselves of their 88 pounds of deadly kit. Most of them managed to slip it off and swim ashore, but several of them succumbed to the overpowering burden and were drawn down before they could get rid of it.

So as the ten remaining craft came ashore, the survivors of the other four followed, somehow swimming in heavy boots and sodden uniforms. Nearly one-third of the total force lost their weapons and other equipment, and until they could capture some, they were without any means of defending themselves. They could only dash for the assembly point and wait there for whatever came.

The force was already seriously depleted, but now the Germans in Le Hamel and elsewhere set up an enfilading crossfire. Before the Commandos could get away, they were a badly depleted troop. Worse was to follow. According to plan their first rendezvous, the village of La Rossière, should have been taken by the 30th Corps, but the Germans still held it. The only course open was to go straight through, which they proceeded to do, the two leading troops running right into the village firing at all defended houses. Panes of glass shattered, bullets filled the air, and soon the Germans rushed out in surrender, hands behind helmets.

By-passing Arromanches, they fought through orchards between blossom and greenness, and across fields broken by patterns of hedges and ditches till at last the Commandos looked up to see Hill 72, a prominent landmark two miles south of Port-en-Bessin, near the Bayeux road.

Their encounters with the enemy had helped them in one way, by providing enough extra weapons to replace those lost in the landing. But the situation seemed far from in hand. They were several hours behind their schedule and completely isolated. The port was known to be strongly garrisoned, and in addition a German fortified camp stood only a mile away from them to the south of the hill. Furthermore, they could only hope to capture the port with the aid of a previous naval bombardment, and this had to be ordered and directed by radio. Now a count showed that three of the Commandos' four sets were lost and the one remaining was either permanently or temporarily out of order. Without it, nothing could be gained. But now, as the sun set, they had to rest— and try to repair their only link with the Allies at sea. Tired out after their fantastic day, they slept, not knowing what the next day might bring.

The fanatical German defense of Le Hamel could not be broken until a combined onslaught was aimed at it from land and sea. Under the cover of gunfire from sea, the Hampshires and relief

193

brigades took the Germans on the flank and turned west to Arromanches. First the destroyers shelled the area, then the smaller support craft crept in closer and picked off individual strongpoints which were still firing. Ashore, armored vehicles reached the Arromanches beaches, an important gain as this would soon be the location of one of the two prefabricated Mulberry harbors which were already taking strange shape in various parts of the Channel.

Between the two British assaults on Gold and Sword, the French-Canadians lost a little of their initial impetus as machine-gun and heavier fire halted their sweep south out of Bernières. Then the situation became confused as, about 1130, the follow-up 9th Brigade plunged ashore before the armor already choking the narrow streets of Bernières could be cleared.

The time was noon, and a Bren-gun carrier of this 3rd Canadian Division was driving down the ramp of tank-landing craft N.22.885. Another one was a couple of lengths farther inshore in a foot of water, while the wheels of a third scudded through the muddy sand. Like all other vehicles used in early stages of the invasion, these had been waterproofed so that no matter what depth they were driven into the sea—within reason—they could still run. But this relief armor cluttered up the beaches more and more and by the time it slowly moved into Bernières the vehicles were bumper to bumper. Luckily nothing disastrous occurred through this hold-up, except that time itself was precious on D-Day and if wasted it could never be reclaimed. No fault lay with the Canadians, however. Mainly it was the wreckage on the beach which slowed up progress.

By 1500 the way was comparatively clear again and the Canadian tanks thundered ahead toward their end-of-day target, the Bayeux-Caen road. They reached it, but because the infantry could not keep pace, the tanks actually had to retreat a little!

As evening came, the Canadians met the British near Creully. By now the Gold-Juno beaches ran a respectable width of a dozen miles. But neither there nor inland was land won without desolation, destruction, death.

Even with the 48 and 41 Commandos assaulting between Juno and Sword, these beachheads could not be joined on D-Day

194

itself. The Commandos did their duty well, however, with the help of a remarkable support group, the Royal Marine armored support group which went into action on several beaches, including those earmarked for the 48 and 41 Commandos. They were the first Royal Marines ever to fight in tanks. Landing in Shermans and other tanks, they were intended to operate for only a week to help break the crust of the enemy's coast defenses, but so successful were they that they ultimately advanced ten miles instead of the one originally ordered.

All the morning of D-Day, 48 Commando had fought on the bloody beach of St. Aubin-sur-Mer. Now it had to take Langrune, the fortified defense point, to do which would require not only courage but desperate daring. With the aid of the tanks of the armored support group they stormed the right-hand end but could not hold it. Nevertheless, despite their precarious situation they went straight at the face of this poisonous "hedgehog." Two Canadian guns and a Sherman tank shattered an antitank wall, opening the way for the Commandos to get a footing into the houses along the strongpoint. The Germans could not match the Commandos in hand-to-hand combat and the garrison surrendered. Langrune, strongest of all the German hedgehog defenses, had fallen. Yet again, victory was not gained without losses. From the moment of landing on that shell-shocked strip of beach to the time of surrender, the Commando had lost nearly half its strength. Casualties included all the fighting troop commanders, and four out of the five seconds-in-command of fighting troops.

The adjacent Commandos—No. 41—had ended the morning without the radio they needed, but as if by a miracle they acquired one soon afterward and called up their supporting destroyers for a two-hour softening up of the strongpoint and château. As night fell, the Lincolns and Royal Ulster Rifles reinforced the Commandos and all seemed set for the assault. But the next day as they were poised ready for the final assault, three German Heinkels streaked across the sky, with Spitfires almost on their tails. Diving down with a terrifying screech, the Heinkels released their bombs on the Commando headquarters killing three men outright and wounding nine including Lieutenant Colonel Gray. But the Commandos were used to adversity by now, and fired by this reverse they went on with the Lincolns to encompass and take both the strongpoint and the château by brilliantly executed assaults. And that same evening, their survivors advanced to Luc-sur-Mer and joined up with the half strength left of 48 Commando.

From Luc-sur-Mer to Ouistreham was Sword sector. What was happening on this crucial beach area north of Caen?

Four tin-hatted Tommies of the British 3rd Division sat on a gun carrier speeding off its landing craft towing an antitank gun. On the side of the carrier was chalked the name Seadog. The Panzers had better beware.

At noon the tide still ran high and as the Ulster Rifles poured out of Landing Craft Infantry L 299 they were faced with two immediate problems. The first was how to carry a folding bicycle through fifty feet of sea, holding on with one hand to a rope line attached to the shore. And second, where was the beach? Here it consisted of only a yard or two of crowded sand, so they were soon on the promenade using their bikes. Shells fell around them as they wobbled past seaside houses with holes blown in the roof— or with no roof at all.

In another L.C.I., S 530, French Commandos lined up eagerly as the craft stopped. Then, their berets tilted to one side, they slid down the sides of buckled ramps and in a moment stood on the shore of their own country again; for them all, after an absence of four long years. But there was no time for sentiment. Machine-gun tracers reminded them that though the first attack was over, the battle had barely begun.

No. 4 Commando landed to the left and stormed the west end of Ouistreham to clear out enemy snipers still firing rifles on the beach where the East Yorks landed. Beside the Commandos another of those mysterious Special Service Brigades, the 1st this time, sped in a spearhead aimed due south to relieve the 6th Airborne Division on the Orne since the early hours of the morning.

The East Yorks continued to be harassed all morning. Meanwhile with the tide approaching flood the relief waves of the assault struggled over submerged obstacles prickling with Teller mines. The sappers and frogmen were doing their best but the task of threading through the obstacles, the abandoned assault craft, and other debris was if anything more difficult than that of the first troops. And not only did they have to contend with the enemy—Allied self-propelled guns were by now keeping up a steady stream of firing from the very water's edge! Thus to get ashore, the second waves had to sneak in low so as to be sure and avoid the shells aimed just over the top of the beach at inland positions.

For an hour which seemed longer to the men than any sixty minutes ever before, the enemy artillery laid down an uncannily accurate barrage on the Sword beaches, blasting the fresh British forces at every step. Broadside on to the beach, assault landing craft S 22 swayed crazily with the tide while the body of a British soldier lay nearby, flat on his back, his knuckles bent, his tin hat blown off.

Then someone looked up and realized that the barrage balloons glinting silver-gray over the beaches to prevent German Stukas from dive-bombing the troops were actually responsible for the accuracy of this barrage. At once their lines were cut and they sauntered along the line of the coast blown by the stiff west-north-west wind.

This did not mean that balloons failed to give their unique protection against low-flying air attacks, or have their well-known morale value to the troops operating beneath them. In fact the whole question of where and when to fly the barrage balloons marked just one more large detail in the over-all operation.

The services agreed that ships would benefit from the balloons, but that they must not be allowed to give away positions. The ultimate compromise was that balloons should be flown at 100 feet not less than seven miles behind the early assault. But this height is the worst possible at which they could fly, for a balloon is inclined to react to air currents by diving down from such a low altitude. Despite this, they were successfully flown at the required 100 feet. To get the total 285 balloons required for the beach areas into the air, a method had to be devised to fly two balloons from each L.S.T. It required some time before the technique for this was achieved, but at last on D-Day quite an impressive force took the balloons across and sustained them with the necessary hydrogen and replacements.

Historians have already recorded the strange facts that follow about the advance from Sword beach during the day. But one fact is obvious: so much stress had been laid on the initial assault that the men inevitably tended to be unable to think beyond the beaches. And according to some informed commentators like Chester Wilmot a defensive mentality was unduly prominent among some of the senior commanders. Wilmot has pointed out particularly that the commander of the 8th Brigade was ill-cast for the role of pursuit.

The South Lancs, for instance, took Hermanville but then dug in there instead of advancing farther to their objective of Périers Rise. The 1st Suffolk, too, seemed slow in capturing Colleville. Yet when their artillery began to fire ranging shots on an enemy battery position due to be taken, sixty-seven Germans hurried out with their hands up! While the infantry were moving more slowly, No. 4 Commando had streaked straight through Colleville to the Orne, where they kept a late lunchtime appointment at 1330 with the 6th Airborne. The sun had set before the infantry reached the same spot.

Meanwhile the forces for the direct thrust on Caen were gathered among the orchards of Hermanville by 1100. The idea was for them to ride the tanks down the main road, but at noon both the tanks and supporting artillery still stood on the beach in a frustrating traffic jam. Time ticked by quickly as the vehicles slowly got away, and then came the further complication of enemy interference on one flank of the infantry's assembly area. At last, with the tanks still not available, the Norfolks and Suffolks could not risk any further delay and had to take parallel routes on foot and hope to be followed by the tanks. The aim of capturing Caen on D-Day was already fading fast, but there were some compensations; the opposition here had not been as heavy as expected. The only pity was that they failed to extract the fullest advantage from

198

this good fortune. In fact, Caen was not destined to fall for a long time yet.

So the beaches still formed the focus. Even though the gunfire became less intense, the future fate of Europe lay along those narrow sands and stones. But by now there were a few early signs of success: a tank moving south up a beach, and two dusty Germans, hands raised with a rifle barrel behind them, walking north in its tracks, smearing the sandy pattern.

Heavy Sherman tanks rolled in, carrying such unlikely things as a motorcycle and rider. Gradually the beaches were becoming organized now and the tanks swung round parallel to the land and trundled off in single file.

All along the beaches, as the crash and clamor subsided a little, the flotsam remained. Among it the sappers moved steadily with their detectors, searching for mines, making them safe. Crab tanks helped too, their metallic flails pawing through the sand. And here and there in their haste the Germans had helped by leaving the telltale skull and crossbones sign MINEN on posts! Salvage men decided which of the damaged landing craft could be removed by sea, which would have to be shifted ashore. Naval Beachmasters from the Mediterranean campaigns prepared the way for the follow-up convoys to come.

And always the fantastic refuse of battle. Gas masks, water bottles, khaki in all shapes. Behind barbed wire, a deserted German strongpoint with its slits in the thick concrete. And right in front of it on the upper soft sands, the bodies of men. Men who died on D-Day, June 6, 1944. The aching aftermath.

If I should die. . . .

Many had never heard that line or even of Rupert Brooke. Yet there they were, inert, their duty done. A young naval officer by the shore swallowed as he saw them, and knew that this was a moment he would remember all his life. Fifteen years, fifty years.

A shell jerked him back to reality as it sent damp sand flying across the shore. Through the afternoon, with its activity and occasional firing, they began to bury the men.

A hundred different scenes. Special tracks were soon being laid over which the armored vehicles could drive more easily; war correspondents interviewed troops having their first breather so they could tell the world what had been happening; German prisoners waited in the water to be taken across the Channel; guards peered inland through field glasses at the enemy position; men occupied trenches only deserted by the enemy an hour earlier; the Hindenburg bastion repainted *Under New Management* with its new tenants, Sergeant Savage and a crew of Chindits with a Bofors gun; everywhere a five-minute smoke as a reward for and celebration of still being alive; and a more practical expression of it as a beach clearance party found a full jar of naval rum bobbing about among the deadly X-shaped steel obstacles. Up spirits. They gulped down a generous ration of it from a white tin mug and then went back to tasks which suddenly seemed less harrowing. Nearby a naval officer was withdrawing the fangs from a Teller mine atop an X-obstacle.

High and dry on an American beach, three tank-landing ships stood stranded by the ebbing tide, their exit doors opened and their cargo gone, leaving a void in their bows like some featureless face.

Wafting across every beach all afternoon were the bitter tang of stale explosives and the strong smell of the burning wood from the rafters of a hundred houses which stood bleakly abandoned between the opposing forces.

Everywhere now the support men were taking over. Field phones linked the hard-won beaches. And the wounded were being treated. Ever since the cataclysm of the barrage and the landings, the medical corps had followed the men. Doctors swiftly jabbed morphine into urgent cases, as tents sprang up under the shelter of trees and anything else and surgeons set about essential emergency operations or other treatment. The surgeons, like the frogmen, had the double difficulty of doing a delicate job while under enemy fire. Having to operate at all under tent conditions was bad enough, but knowing all the time that the ground—and their hands—might shake in the middle of the operation made their task even tenser. One jolt to an instrument could mean a life lost.

So wherever possible the wounded were evacuated. "Ducks," or DUKWs, barely visible in the waves, chugged inshore on a dual mission: to bring in fresh food and carry out the wounded to waiting ships. Medical corpsmen carried the serious cases on stretchers down the beaches, and soon they were safe aboard the hospital ships heading home.

V for victory—and valor.

And as the wounded lay on their stretchers gazing up at the canvas covers of the DUKWs rolling northward, the convoys of support craft passed them on the way in. After the L.C.A.s, L.C.I.s, L.C.T.s, came the L.C.F.s, L.C.S.s, L.C.G.s, the landing ships, headquarters ships, more DUKWs and Rhino craft.

All the small support craft were manned by marines, and presented an amazing array of designs: including flat-bottomed, flatnosed Landing Craft Vehicles, under 37 feet long and among the smallest to steam across the Channel under their own power. Landing Craft Mechanized were little larger. With the perilous voyage over, these L.C.M.s and L.C.V.s began weeks of work as sea taxis in every kind of condition. Tanks, trucks, guns, ammunition and food—all had to be ferried across to wherever they were needed most, and always the craft would be exposed to attack by air or sea.

Vehicles were transferred from parent ships to Rhino barges to be brought to the beaches. That first afternoon, one of the few successes the enemy had was to set on fire a Rhino while it was actually alongside its parent vessel. They were in the middle of lowering the vehicles from the ship to the Rhino—so named for its likeness to the animal—and the fire quickly spread the length of the craft which was already half-loaded with gasoline-filled vehicles and threatened to explode at any moment. Then in a split second, a group of Royal Marines clambered down into the flaming barge and somehow succeeded in first transferring all the wounded to the parent ship and then forcing the blazing barge away from the vessel's side.

This was one of a thousand unsung sidelights of the invasion.

Sidelights such as L.C.T. 921 which, her task of landing vehicles done, turned to clear the way for others in those crowded waters. For an hour or two, her return voyage was as uneventful as the trip south. Then suddenly a torpedo erupted volcanically on her port side near the wheelhouse. Spray spurted over the deck as in the middle of a monsoon. A man fell before the blast. The metal hull and casing crumpled as if made of cardboard leaving a great gap through which the sea splashed in. Frantically the crew bunged the leaks and sailed her on. The deck had actually been rolled up, leaving the metal-supporting girders exposed. Riding lower in the water, L.C.T. 921 sailed slowly north and sighted the Isle of Wight before dark. When she finally rounded the island and crept back to a berth in Southampton Water, no one in the little semi-detached houses lining the coast noticed her obscure outline.

She had returned damaged, but with honor. Overhead two hundred and fifty transports towing gliders droned across the sunset sky on their way to the beachhead. But before these relief airborne forces dropped on France the original men of the 6th Airborne Division were still struggling to hold their bridges.

Eighteen

DAWN on D-Day, and the 7th Battalion of the British 5th Parachute Brigade defending their bridge over the Canal de Caen began to be bothered by locals, French civilians made apprehensive by the Allied air bombardment, who wished to get out from the area which they rightly assumed would soon become a battleground. Not all the French desired to leave, however, and the matron of a maternity clinic at the Château de Benouville remained at her post throughout the invasion to see several babies born within the sounds of both Allied and German guns.

Wherever they were that early morning, the various battalions of the 5th Brigade felt isolated amidst a host of enemy. Then the sound of exploding shells as the Allies began their pre-attack bombardment cheered them. Soon they would be no longer on their own in this no man's land between two massive armies.

At 0715 the shelling stopped abruptly. This the paratroopers knew meant that the first wave of the assault was nearing the beaches. But until the first infantrymen arrived, it was obvious that the Germans would keep the airborne vanguard dangerously occupied. Inevitably casualties mounted as German snipers picked off odd paratroops from various vantage points. Fire came from every conceivable direction, and no place was sacred, not even a nearby church tower, which was obviously sheltering several snipers. Eventually a bomb from a paratrooper's Piat scored a bull's-eye on the tower and a dozen Germans were killed. But while the paratroopers were not troubled again from that particular source, casualties continued hour by hour and a steady stream of wounded made their way to an aid station set up in a café by the bridge of Le Port.

Three more hours passed, and then at about 1000 the guards on the bridge spotted a pair of red-beret-topped figures striding toward the bridge. When challenged they turned out to be none other than Brigadier Gale himself, and Brigadier Kindersley whose Air Landing Brigade was not due to land until the evening of D-Day. In the meantime both brigadiers were checking up on the all-vital paratroop position.

The two officers had hardly arrived when two boats hove into view, clearly making for Caen. The paratroopers opened fire with a Bren gun and another precious Piat. Projectiles from both hit on the nearer boat, which went drifting aimlessly across the canal until it jolted against the bank, whereupon its German army crew voluntarily forfeited their active interest in the rest of the war. Seeing the fate of the first boat, the commander of the second changed course and fled toward the sea.

Twelve hours which seemed like twelve days had passed now since the paratroopers had floated down through the chill night air, and the effect of those twelve hours of constant turmoil began to be felt about noon. This was the ideal hour psychologically, therefore, for the men to hear the distant skirl of bagpipes. Never had they sounded so sweet to men not born in Scotland!

"They're coming!" a corporal called, voicing the feelings of all those guarding the bridge. Then, despite snipers, the first troops reached the paratroopers and everywhere there were quick handshakes. These first arrivals were the Commandos, who had charged wildly through Colleville. Then at 1400 hours, the pipers of Lord Lovat's 1st Special Service Brigade marched over the bridge, the shrill of their instruments drowning out the sounds of mortar shells and small-arms fire. And thus it was that this vital point, seized and held safe for the invaders, was later christened Pegasus Bridge in honor of the paratroops who wear the insignia of a flying horse.

But the thrill of the link-up did not last for long, for it was just one more incident in a day crowded with memories. In Benouville itself, A Company of the 7th Battalion had been having a bad time ever since it had been attacked from three sides before dawn. No real reinforcements could get through to the company until early evening, when word came back that all its officers had been killed or wounded, but it still held its position. For seventeen hours the company fought on almost continuously, and at one point a German attack reached the regimental aid post before it was repulsed. In the confusion of the moment, however, Chaplain George Parry was killed, a casualty which brought real grief to each man in the company.

All day it was touch and go with A Company. Then finally relief reached them. As the sun sank in the west and scattered clouds covered much of the sky, the great glider force scheduled for that evening flocked overhead—on time and in the right order and place. The graceful gliders settled down like giant birds of prey swooping earthward. Gradually their massive frames settled onto a wheat field which was one of the prepared positions. A few missed the actual field, but most came to rest within mere yards of each other— very different from the previous night's drop. For twenty hours the paratroops had held the bridges over the Orne and the Canal de Caen. Now relief had come from the skies.

Then about 2000 hours, the seaborne relief also broke through, so that the paratroopers' long vigil was really over, at least for the moment. But with the land link-up came a sudden sharp reminder that the war was still very much in progress. A lone German Fock-Wulf 190 flew in almost at ground level and dropped a large bomb on the precious bridge over the canal. But fortunately it somehow failed to explode!

Lieutenant Colonel Pine-Coffin now ordered his men across the canal toward Ranville, although he himself stayed behind until the dial of his luminous wrist watch showed 0100 on June 7. A whole day had passed since he first had felt French soil beneath him, and the bridge was still safe in Allied hands. When the last man was settled down he followed his men and caught a few hours' sleep.

D-Day with the 12th Battalion found a special naval officer dropped with the airborne men contacting an Allied cruiser by radio so that it could bring its guns to bear on targets north of the battalion around Ouistreham. Captain J. A. N. Sim and a few paratroops were with the officer some 300 yards in front of the main paratroop positions covering the village of Le Bas de Ranville. As the gray light of early morning filtered through the branches of the surrounding trees they glimpsed a group of unidentifiable men approaching. They seemed to be British airborne, although at the distance it was impossible to be certain.

Sim, however, suddenly realized that they were Germans—and that there were a great many of them. Here was exactly the kind of emergency that the airborne men had to be ready to meet in the van of an invasion. There was no time to ask for orders from behind. Waiting till the Germans were little more than fifty yards away, Sim whispered a command—and a Verey light hissed into the air toward the approaching foe. It fell right among the Germans, silhouetting their bodies against the lightening sky.

Instinctively the Germans fell to the ground as the paratroops opened a rapid fire. The British at first had the element of surprise, but soon the advantage was lost as two 88-mm. guns, advancing close behind the German infantry, were brought into play. Two paratroopers were killed almost at once while the naval officer received a bad bullet wound in the thigh, which put him out of action.

The little force held on for what seemed a long, long time as, under cover of the two 88's, the Germans began to crawl round their right flank in an obvious effort to set up a cross fire. Then a shell from a German mortar burst immediately above the hedge sheltering them. The situation deteriorated dramatically. Now only four of the fourteen were alive and unwounded: Sim, his batman, and two sergeants, Jones and Millburn. Still the Englishmen returned the Germans' fire, but now Sim realized that to stay there longer would obviously mean the end of them all. The hedge could not be held.

Sim decided to withdraw. So the four fit men helped the wounded to their feet and they all set out for the company's main position via a shallow ditch. All the way back they presented targets for the Germans, who were no more than a hundred yards away at the beginning. Yet somehow, the survivors returned to the main British position, through that 300 yards of hell. Sim was not beaten, however, and later returned to the very same hedge with reinforcements. C Company's antitank guns had accounted for the Germans'

88-mm. weapons by this time, so things were easier. And this time they held the hedge.

Sergeants Jones and Millburn were both awarded the Distinguished Conduct Medal, but both were killed later. Sim received the Military Cross.

Meanwhile the 13th Battalion of the 5th Parachute Brigade, having cleared Ranville earlier, proceeded to help in the task of preparing landing fields for the gliders due later in the day. But one party of about twenty men of the 13th under a Captain Kerr became separated from the battalion and spent D-Day in the rather remote Bois de Bavent. By midafternoon they were exhausted after crossing several waterways and were deep in the tidal marshes. Then just as the men felt they would have to rest, they saw their relief gliders dipping gracefully in to land. This brought the first cheer of the day, to be followed soon after by another as a squadron of Spitfires shot down two enemy fighters, which crashed into the marsh quite near them. It took them six hours to traverse two miles of this marshland. Their goal was Le Mesnil, and the day ended as a Frenchman, who had apparently lost no time in celebrating the liberation, gave them somewhat incoherent directions for getting there.

Southeast of Ranville, the 8th Battalion of the 3d Parachute Brigade was having an adventurous time. Some of the men dropped a considerable distance from the scheduled drop zone and had brief brisk encounters with the enemy. A few even floated down near the other brigade at Ranville, and were temporarily taken prisoner by a local garrison. The Germans found it difficult to hold paratroops for long, however. They caught one man, a Sergeant Jones, for instance, but he managed to seize a gun and shoot eight Germans dead before escaping.

By this kind of extreme endeavor, 230 men of the 8th Battalion reached the outskirts of the Bois de Bavent. Under the circumstances, Lieutenant Colonel Pearson in command considered himself fortunate to have this many men with him, yet he knew he must create the impression that he had a far greater force. Thus he at once organized a series of patrols. He himself led the first of these and made an attempt to rescue any possible survivors from a Dakota they had heard crash near the woods. Crossing the River Dives, he left part of the patrol to guard the dinghy the patrol had used. Eventually they reached a small village well behind the German lines close to the area where they thought the Dakota had crashed. Advancing through it, Pearson and a few others approached a farmhouse beyond it. Eventually they reappeared pulling a cart bearing eight wounded men from the aircraft whom they got safely back to their main force.

Now to the north, the 1st Canadian Parachute Battalion was remedying the unfortunate situation caused by a drop so badly scattered that one group of men actually fell west of the River Orne several miles away. Despite these difficulties in the V landing sector, the Canadians took Varaville as planned and destroyed the bridge in the town. Bringing their trusty Piats to bear, they then exchanged bitter fire with the garrison of a pillbox until 1030 when the Germans surrendered.

At the same time, other Canadians were seizing Robehomme near the River Dives. As with other airborne detachments, they had sappers with them for the specialized job of demolishing key strongpoints. And here it was that Captain A. J. Jack of the Royal Engineers enhanced the sappers' reputation for courageous eccentricity—or eccentric courage—by blowing up the bridge and then sitting down with his men in the middle of the village to cook and eat a delayed breakfast! The local French were quick to tell them that the enemy might appear at any moment yet were clearly impressed by this unintentional display of calm.

Still farther north, the victorious 9th Battalion, flushed from their triumph in silencing the almost legendary Merville battery, now advanced to their second task of taking a patch of high ground. Soon they met a Frenchman who warned them that a little village on their route was held by two hundred Germans. It was now full daylight and Colonel Otway called a halt. The position to be attacked was a small château, loopholed for defense, and surrounded by a stone wall six feet high. It was clearly too strong to overrun without artillery or air support, so the battalion took up a defensive position opposite from which they prevented the enemy from moving to the Orne and the areas of the invasion which was now gathering momentum. Snipers badly harassed the parachutists who were by now so few that there had to be an interval of ten yards between each man. It was a thin line indeed, but one which held until help came next day from the Commandos who went on to capture the German position.

Finally over to the west the American paratroops were engaged in a desperate struggle for their lives throughout D-Day and had to leave bridges unblown. But they did secure the exits to the causeways across the notorious swamps. And as they struggled, often in ones or twos, the American glider pilots gradually wound their way through the German—and Allied—lines back to the beaches, and so back by sea for reinforcements. Reaching the safety of a landing craft, they smoked a cigarette, leaned on their guns, and swapped stories of how they had got there. Now it was up to others for a while.

Nineteen

THERE was no doubt now but that the outer crust of Hitler's West Wall had been breached. But as D-Day drew to an end the overpowering impetus of the initial assault had begun to be lost, and all along the coast expectations turned to counter-attack. Some of this was just natural reaction: the recoil after the fury of that first amazing morning. But the Germans actually were grouping to try and counterattack. Rommel himself moved up behind Caen as Montgomery landed to find his advance head-quarters. So the old enemies were facing each other again—and at pretty close range. German infantry were on the move toward the Americans in an attempt to cut them off from the rest of the beach-head, while the Panzers and SS troops poised to strike at the British and Canadians.

Two dozen Panzer tanks tried to drive a wedge between the latter two late on D-Day, but by this time our own DD and other tanks were inland, supported by mobile guns. After a slugging match of shells, the Panzers clumsily turned in their tracks and headed south, leaving five of the twenty-four smoking ruins. A second Panzer attack scheduled later in the evening was forestalled to the hour by the advance of the first paratroops and relief forces from the bridgehead.

Meanwhile the most vivid memories of the day were personal ones: each man's own fight multiplied a hundred thousand times. Or to be precise, by D-Day and D+1, 176,475 times. A major driving gaily in a captured 10 h.p. car; a captured truck loaded with still-hot soup, coffee and fresh bread for a phantom enemy unit; cigars by the box and wine by the barrel; dead cows in a field, their legs sticking strangely in the air; a fearful flash as a German mortar hits an ammunition truck, and one thinks of the driver inside; the first night and in a tank harbor still-helmeted men write home or just fold their arms and fall asleep; four men carrying their wounded company sergeant major to a forward field dressing station; motorcyclists resting beside their vehicles on the edge of a road; a mine-hunting Labrador dog, Jasper, has his head bandaged after receiving a wound to his right ear; an old Frenchman unfurls a faded tricolor from his balcony as slates fall off the roof; a Tommy carries a trophy, a MINEN sign left by the Germans in their haste; another one has a sign ready to plant in a cleared path NO MINES; sappers sweeping for mines in the ruined square of Tilly-sur-Seulles; and four forlorn prisoners walking in front of a private with a Sten gun.

It is night now, but there is little sleep. Often the enemy infantry were only two or three hundred yards ahead, and black-faced patrols crisscrossed no man's land throughout the night. Stabs of light as guns fired or grenades burst, then quiet. With day came the big guns again, making the efforts of the individual infantryman seem almost pointless; yet it was armor and men together which would win or lose the battle of Normandy.

In all this confusion mistakes were inevitable. Men of the Ulster Rifles, bicycles now abandoned for the most part, edged along a copse when without warning tracer fired by their own supporting tanks tore at them. It was not always easy to recognize uniforms from a moving tank and across smoke-filled fields. Caught unaware, the Ulsters were in chaos for a few minutes, but fortunately suffered few casualties.

Next day the tanks made up for it fully as they remained with the riflemen all the time they advanced through what seemed a barrage no man could survive. The Ulsters crouched behind or on the flanks of the tanks as they brought their guns to bear on the source of the barrage. And somehow they got through. While this was going on, too, the Canadians threatened to outflank Caen, until halted temporarily by elite German storm troopers.

D+1 and back to the Commandos. The one Commando force not to go into operation until after D-Day was No. 46. Originally scheduled to land in the evening of D-Day to raid two enemy batteries, after arriving off St. Aubin at 1830 they learned at 2200 that both raids were postponed.

At 0600 next morning, the entire plan was altered. Now they received orders to land at once and take the strongpoint at Petit-Enfer. Under the leadership of Lieutenant Colonel Campbell Hardy they were ready by 0900, and landing unopposed they carried out their task with the aid of a naval bombardment and tanks of the Royal Marine armored support unit. Pushing on the same evening, the Commando occupied the small town of La Délivrande two miles inland, where stunned villagers watched tanks roar through their little streets.

Before following 46 Commando units' further adventures toward the end of the week, we must move along the coast to take up again the thrilling assault of 47 Commando on the fortified Port-en-Bessin.

As night fell on D-Day they had been trying to repair their one remaining radio. By morning the signalers had done it and Lieutenant Colonel Phillips launched his plan to take the port. He called on the Royal Navy for a bombardment of the place at 1500 on D+1 day, to be closely followed by a strike from R.A.F. Typhoons at 1550. Then ten minutes later at four o'clock the Royal Artillery were requested to lay a smoke screen.

Each of these requests was carried out to the minute. First the low-pitched rumble of naval guns echoed across the water and reached the ears of the Commandos near Hill 72. Next the Typhoons screamed down strafing the little port with their rocket projectiles. At 1600 the smoke screen appeared dead on cue, and the Commandos dived forward under its cover and stormed into the first strongpoint, just south of the town. The second one, to the west of the harbor, offered stronger resistance but they took this, too, although not without losses. Two German flak ships actually anchored in the harbor turned their guns on the rapidly moving men and killed a number before mortars and Bren guns silenced them. But this delayed the assault of the main strongpoint on a hill east of the harbor.

It was about this time that the Germans in the fortified camp south of Hill 72 went into action. Phillips had left a handful of

Commandos to defend the hill, but when, after a brief bombardment the enemy attacked the hill, they overran the few defenders, and captured it. Darkness was beginning to fall, and now that the Germans held Hill 72 it seemed impossible for the main force to penetrate the mined defenses of the strongpoint that night. Checked in front and threatened from the rear, the Commandos were in a desperate position.

Lieutenant Colonel Phillips was weighing the relative dangers of a night attack on the strongpoint as against waiting until morning when Captain T. F. Cousins reported that he had found a narrow zigzag path up the hill.

"I'm confident that with twenty-five men I can take the strongpoint by surprise," he said to Phillips.

Phillips gave him twice the number of men as well as their one remaining mortar and the promise of support from machine gun. In the gathering dusk, Phillips watched Cousins and his men creep silently up the narrow path till they crossed the skyline and vanished from view. The ensuing eerie silence seemed agonizingly long. Then shouting and the rattle of machine guns reached them. Cousins and his men were in the German positions. Phillips at once sent a second troop to their aid and soon the victory was complete as they captured the German commander and persuaded him to call the rest of the garrison to surrender. Later, too, the flak ships capitulated and Port-en-Bessin was in British hands. Then in the moment of triumph, as they were mopping up the maze of trenches and dugouts forming the strongpoint, one of the enemy resisted and Cousins, at the front of his men, was killed. It was a cruel loss.

During the night, the Commandos made contact with the Americans advancing from Omaha beach and the next day they stormed up Hill 72 to recapture their base. By now, other British forces were coming up from the east, and the Commandos handed over their prize of Port-en-Bessin—the first French port to fall into Allied hands.

Twenty

PORT-EN-BESSIN would be useful, of course, but the overriding need now was for one or preferably two full-scale supply harbors.

These were already on their way across the Channel! The Magnificent Mulberries.

The urgency of this need for a reliable port was being underlined meanwhile on D+1 as the build-up of supplies which were to sustain the bridgehead began. Eight ship convoys were due to arrive on D+1. One of these, consisting of nine large personnel ships, came from the Thames and this Convoy E.T.P.I. was in fact the first group of large ships to pass the Straits of Dover in four years.

While motor launches and aircraft of Fleet Air Arm laid smoke screens to help E.T.P.I. to slip through between Dover and Calais, a motor transport convoy of smaller ships went ahead. Enemy batteries on the French coast picked these up, however, and scored a direct hit on one ship, which sank. Admiral Ramsay now had to decide whether or not to risk a daylight passage for the big ships. The convoy was then ahead of time, so a signal was flashed to it to turn back along the east Kent coast while the motor launches put in to replenish their supplies of smoke. By mid-afternoon, a most effective dense screen hung in the straits and at 1700 on D-Day E.T.P.I. put on full speed and passed through without any enemy interference. Next morning all eight convoys were at their proper places off the Normandy coast, and began unloading. At midday, however, the wind from the north reached a strength of well over 15 m.p.h. and unloading became extremely difficult. Everything cried out for the sheltered water of a harbor.

Let us go back forty-eight hours now as the sixty Gooseberry blockships steamed slowly up Channel past *Warspite, Ramillies, Dragon, Frobisher, Danae, Aurora, Mauritius.*

"Serial 1 in force," signaled the flagship. That meant D-Day was June 6, and H-Hour 0720.

But exact timing was not yet vital.

"Speed six knots," signaled *Alynbank,* as they literally plowed east-northeast, anxiously watching the weather all day. Away to the south they saw the comforting sleekness of six patrolling destroyers, while overhead four Hurricanes flew.

The sea was crowded as daylight showed the same white-crested wave tops. Portland Bill lay on the port beam now and the sea seemed full of minesweepers: the ships which would soon be sweeping those ten vital channels south.

The blockships anchored in Poole Bay as the wind blew over the dusty beaches of Sandbanks. They were waiting now only for confirmation that Serial 1 had not been canceled.

Then came a signal from the fluttering flags:

"Open package A."

The waiting ships learned at last what would be required of them.

"The ships are to be scuttled off the enemy coast to form a breakwater giving shelter to the beaches on which the army has landed, and for the landing craft which will be using those beaches for landing stores and troops in support of the assault. The channels will all have been swept but it is important that ships shall not stray outside the channels as the surrounding water is mined."

Now they had only to wait. Spume splintered at the wave tops as the little minesweepers began their grim task, and left the Gooseberry ships in peace for the night. From the blockships they saw a convoy of coasters weigh anchor in the evening, yet it was still all rather hard to believe. Now, as darkness fell, the lines of landing craft began their silent run from the Solent and elsewhere, and soon the blockships were left almost alone as an unreal silence came with the end of the day. Surely this could not be the beginning of an armada which made the Spanish one seem so small?

Yet the evidence was all there. The old British battleship *Centurion* plodded up to the Corncob convoy of Gooseberry just before nightfall. She had come all the way from the Mediterranean and looked almost as if she were exhausted from the trip. The last thing Lieutenant Commander Taylor in *Durban* remembered that night was drowsing off to the drone of our bombers. And the first thing the next morning—D-Day—the steward was saying:

"Seven o'clock, sir; in twenty minutes they'll be touching down on the beaches."

Even the steward knew. Soon the world would rejoice. But now the old ships had their duty to do. A strange, sad job that would be their last. Taylor saw the French battleship *Courbet* and nearby several merchant ships launched as long ago as 1903. After forty-one years this was to be their end. Yet how much more honorable than the breaker's yard?

Slowly now they weighed anchor. The waves had little effect on the British and Dutch cruisers, *Durban* and *Sumatra,* but the smaller ships felt them, as they piled over the bows.

From a radio in the cabin came brief news of the invasion.

On the upper deck of *Sumatra* the men were issuing brown boxes of emergency rations as *Durban* steamed past her. For no one quite knew what would happen over there.

They had time to spare. During the afternoon they reached Area Z, coded as Piccadilly Circus. All approach channels led to Z buoy, and all traffic must pass round it to reach one of the five channels which pointed to Normandy like outstretched fingers, to break into ten channels farther south.

From three sides of the compass, craft converged on Area Z, with its buoy at the center of its five-mile circle of water swept clear of mines.

Here they spent hours zigzagging to waste time, for Z buoy must not be rounded before midnight. Meanwhile the sea was filled with silent ships creeping secretly toward each dim navigational mark. Radar was the only exactitude. To starboard of *Durban,* a convoy

217

of landing ships forced Corncob convoy to the eastward of where their channel lay in passing at a higher speed. And although the channels had all been swept once, six sweepers ahead suddenly fired a mine, turning night briefly into day. Another mine. And another. So the way was not necessarily plain sailing. But there were those who welcomed the threat of danger. For many sailors in Corncob and the D-Day escorts, things had been "bloody boring," as one man expressed it.

First light on D+1 revealed that *Durban* had drifted until they did not know which of the five channels she occupied! Nor whether they would see the coast of Arromanches or Vierville. Other ships in the Gooseberry force had split into their groups and were sailing sedately down different channels. But at least all bows pointed one way . . . roughly. The night had been full of the sound of aircraft, now as D+1 dawned the droning redoubled. It was a welcome noise. But the weather was less welcome. The sea was still rough, the sky unpromising and sullen.

Then out of the half light a craft came reeling toward *Durban,* which narrowly missed colliding with her as she floated out of the gray gloom. At first she appeared to be abandoned, but then someone signaled from her by semaphore:

"Engine flooded." And she spun crazily away again.

Now as the light grew, the *Durban*'s crew watched the passing pageant of ships. That strip of land known to them only as the Far Shore lay dead ahead now. And a vast fleet lay off it. Taylor thought it impossible that so many ships could conceivably have crossed the Channel in one day—yet there they were.

He looked to the right, to the American sector, and saw a large troop transport ablaze. Omaha was still having a tough time. Red flames were bright at the base of a great column of smoke.

Now it was day again, and the big ships recommenced their bombardment. Six hundred and forty guns had joined in yesterday, and it seemed as if there were at least as many today. This first convoy of 45 blockships arrived in the assault area at 1230. Opposite the *Durban* a dusty haze hung over a line of black dots that snaked over a rise and out of sight. But was it Arromanches or Port-en-Bessin?

Alynbank seemed sure anyway.

"Have contacted surveyor," she told them. She had two hours of life left, for she would be the first to go. The Planter was there to plant the blockships exactly where they ought to go. Precision was important.

Durban did not see *Alynbank*'s end. Suddenly her skipper saw that two tugs were not where they should have been behind *Durban*. They must have gone astray during the night when the convoy was split. So *Durban* dashed off—as fast as she was able—and found them riding quietly at anchor five miles away. Like two lost children, they were waiting for someone to tell them where to go next!

Durban told them. Then racing back toward the scuttling zone, the ship found that the army was still running into unexpectedly heavy resistance ashore and had called on support from the warships. Across the water came the regulated, disciplined crack of six-inch guns from *Nelson, Mauritius, Danae* and *Dragon,* whom the Gooseberries had seen so lately off the Dorset coast. *Durban* passed *Sumatra* and the second convoy, the Dutch ship passing in a faint secretive hum of machinery. Homeward-bound traffic sailing north dotted the scene.

Then before the blockships could maneuver in position to be sunk, the Germans launched air and sea attacks in the area. During the previous night, June 6-7, German R-boats ventured out of Le Havre while other E-boats sailed from the western port of Cherbourg. The first night the strong Allied coastal forces at once intercepted them and inflicted damage to several before the Germans veered round and fled back home again. But the next night the attack was repeated, and the Luftwaffe also roused itself to try to attack the beaches and shipping. This raid of June 7-8 was not serious but unluckily one of the early attacks soon after midnight coincided with the arrival of a number of Allied aircraft carrying airborne reinforcements. The Dakotas carrying these troops were fired on by ships of the Eastern Task Force and at least one Dakota was shot down with the loss of crew and paratroops.

This encounter marked the beginning of the battle of the Seine Bay which was fought by the entire Allied navy with every kind of craft. By day, during these early D, D+1 and D+2 days, the German coastal guns blazed away at the battleships and got back more than they gave. By night, the Luftwaffe began to drop parachute mines. And also at night the Germans attacked not only with R-boats and E-boats, but also with such unusual devices as human torpedoes, midget submarines and explosive motorboats—all intended to break up the line of warships and light craft which protected the beaches. This row of craft six miles or so north of the invasion shores was called the Trout Line and its screen extended from the very mouth of the River Orne well out to sea.

Two special kinds of craft, Landing Craft Gun and Landing Craft Flak, L.C.G. and L.C.F., respectively, by the accuracy of their fire were particularly responsible for foiling most of the German lunges on the line. During these first days, they had their first experience with the unmanned high-speed German explosive motorboats. The gun crews had to keep their wits about them to tackle these, for if they were engaged at too great a range the vessel under attack found that the motorboats were still heading straight in when all the magazines were empty. Thus the defending craft often waited till these unnerving boats were within a hundred yards before firing. And several were sunk from even closer quarters.

Inside this screen the *Durban* survived the night of June 7 and the next morning was back where she had been previously. By now her captain had spent fifty-six hours continuously on the bridge.

By the time the entire convoy arrived at the Gooseberry area, *Alynbank* had already been scuttled, but she had gone down so that there was a considerably greater depth of water over her stern than over her bow. She was also badly out of position. She was to have been the key ship for the line to be laid, but she had sunk slowly, listed heavily, and slewed right out of line. It was not surprising, perhaps, since there had been considerable doubt whether the old ships would go down on an even keel. In an effort to try to ensure that they did, they had all been ballasted.

One down, fifty-nine to go.

Then the long line of ships began to go down: to form five and a half miles of breakwater for the two Mulberry harbors. Over in the other area, S.S. *Alymare* settled low, her number in the convoy 504, only a few feet above the water.

Next came *Saltersgate*. After pushing and pulling of tugs, at last the order came:

"Abandon ship."

Bundles were thrown on to a waiting tug; figures scrambled down the ladder. One lone man remained on the poop.

"Stand by aft."

The figure on the poop raised a hand in acknowledgment.

"Fire," called a voice, and the man vanished. The watchers waited, the tugs stopped pulling. Nothing happened. Then the man was on the poop once more.

"Misfire," said someone.

Then the figure on the poop made his way to the secondary firing position by the officers' bathroom. The ship started violently, then vanished behind a fog of dust thrown up by the ballast. Only the topmasts above the haze told that a ship was still there. And slowly as the haze thinned, the old vessel heeled to port and began to sink slowly. Six minutes passed before the water stopped creeping up her side.

"She's had it," said a young signalman insensitively.

The sun shone brightly now with the warmth of high noon.

"What's for lunch?" came the inevitable query.

The answer was emergency rations of compressed sweetened oatmeal, two blocks of dehydrated meat, four small cakes of beef extract, biscuits, three bars of chocolate, a handful of sweets, and four cubes which were a combination of tea, sugar and milk. A vile liquid could be brewed from these cubes without much effort.

Then on with the job. Gooseberry Four lay ahead. Two ships had been sunk and the third was being maneuvered into position. On the doomed ship, a long cube of corned beef lay ready for slicing and the pots simmered on the stove.

Gooseberry Five was also taking shape. Four vessels sunk and craft already being sheltered on the landward side. First fruits.

Now *Durban* waited at anchor close to *Sumatra*. Soon it would be their turn to be planted. But now a fire fight between the shore batteries and the guns of the supporting fleet reminded them that this was more than a mere exercise. It was a strange sensation, being in the midst of a slugging match between giant guns. But the blockships were too close to shore for them to find it diverting.

Ashore, a great volume of dense smoke, orange at the base, went mushrooming up and up. Then German shells, from far inland now, found a newly landed ammunition dump, and exploding bullets traced fantastic patterns of light on the backdrop of smoke. The Luftwaffe flew over *singly*: how the mighty had fallen.

Now Lieutenant Commander Taylor left the *Durban* by launch to meet the captain of the *Courbet,* a faded French warship which had escaped to Portsmouth in 1940.

"I must go ashore to gather a handful of French soil," the French captain said passionately. Taylor promised he would forward the request. Then back aboard his ship, he slept through the rattle of guns for the rest of the night.

The *Courbet*'s time drew near. Her great size meant she lacked maneuverability, but considerable dignity pervaded her ponderous advance in the eerie dawn light. High up, from the topmost point, a gigantic Free French flag flaunted its colors. At the stern hung a huge tricolor.

Then the Germans started to shell the area as four tugs towed the *Courbet* forward as quickly as they could. At last her bow came to rest on that of another ship already sunk. There was a great rending and tearing of steel, followed by a sudden explosion. There was a dull thud and a brief tremor, then she quickly settled the three feet that separated her keel from the sea bed. The *Courbet* was home—after fourteen years.

One by one they followed in seemingly endless succession. The *Sumatra* steamed into position: it was a sad moment for the Dutch crew of a vessel which had been flagship on an East Indies station for many years. Sadly her crew gathered in the bows and the charges were fired.

222

Shells from the shore straddled the *Durban* now. She might well go down before they could scuttle her in the right spot unless they hurried. Slowly her captain steamed her close to the *Sumatra*. Then there was a violent explosion and slowly she began to settle as her crew wandered about the deck aimlessly. There was no further purpose in their presence.

Soon sixty ships lay off Normandy with only their funnels, masts, and superstructure showing like some strange stunted fleet, half marine, half submarine. They were an ill assortment of shapes and sizes but the sea was smooth on their landward side. Planes passing overhead saw with amazement how the sea was suddenly calmed as its force was broken by the long line of vessels.

Now the task of creating the inner installations to make Mulberry A and B—two harbors each the size of the one at Gibraltar—began.

The harbors would consist of outer floating breakwaters, inner fixed breakwaters of concrete caissons, and floating piers running from the pierheads to the shore. The vast towing task had started on D-Day as innumerable tugs emerged with the results of the work of 15,000 men. Just as the invasion was by far the biggest ever, and the minesweeping and other constituent operations were also all the largest of their kind, so Mulberry was the greatest tow in history. From Sussex and the Solent emerged masses of floating ironmongery, as well as the fabulous Phoenix creations. These concrete giants varied in weight from 1,500 to 6,000 tons, according to the position in which they were to be sunk, and in all 146 had been constructed in eight months.

By the time the last blockships were settling, these concrete caissons were approaching to the invasion scene. The first Phoenix and Whale units and the inner Bombardon breakwaters arrived off the far shore on the morning of D+2. Placing the Phoenix caissons was extremely tricky. The tide had to be slack and the wind light, which was like asking for the moon that week. And when the sea cocks were opened, the tugs had to guide the concrete monsters with absolute accuracy as they sank to the bottom. Any mistakes could be catastrophic. Luckily the tugs were handled skillfully by their American masters and the first of one and a half million tons of gear for the two Mulberries went into place.

The Whale floating roadway units fared less well even before they reached the end of their sea trip. The strong wind was, of course, quite unfavorable for cross-Channel towing and there were a number of crises as the unwieldy Whales fought the struggling crews of the tugs. The result was that 40 per cent of the Whale roadways were lost, including several damaged near the beaches upon arrival, while 60 per cent arrived safely.

The Bombardons arrived more or less intact, to be positioned by a fleet of carriers, net layers, and boom defense vessels. The first lay actually took place on D+1, before the blockships were sunk, and by D+5 the complete floating breakwater at Mulberry A—off Omaha beach—was ready and operating. Within another twenty-four hours the Arromanches Mulberry, too, had all its Bombardons safely moored, although they went much deeper than had been originally intended.

The build-up speeded up greatly as the Mulberries came into use. Already flat-bottom coastal vessels could come right to the beaches, sheltered by the framework of the harbors which were rapidly taking form. Once there, little DUKWs took off vital supplies and sped ashore with them, while the coasters set out on the return voyage to Britain.

Then once the awe-inspiring necklaces of pontoons were in position, carrying floating roadways, the bigger ships steamed in. Through the line of sunken Gooseberry vessels they came, and tied up at the "spud" pierheads, where they were unloaded and their cargoes rushed into vehicles to be driven down the roadways to the shore. At intervals of each one or two hundred feet, the amazing "spuds" rose from the sea itself like torpedoes turned on end.

So there it was. The lines of blockships, bow to stern—or sometimes bow to bow—lay motionless in the swirling tide. And within their shelter, the floating causeways, connecting pierheads with shore, lay scarcely rising or falling on their mesh of metal and the pontoons underneath.

The Mulberries were an amazing achievement in prefabrication. The troops had carried only forty-eight hours' emergency rations to cover D-Day and D+1. Food, ammunition, and all their other supplies had had to be brought in for after that. So the Mulberries were invaluable. Then a week later came the storm.

Twenty-one

DURING that first fortnight, the Gooseberry blockships and the floating breakwaters formed practically the only shelter for the never-ending stream of supply ships, and although the Mulberry projects were even now not yet completed, already vast numbers of men and their stores had passed through these two partial ports.

But the weather continued to be bad and from D+8, June 14, deteriorated steadily until June 18. Even now the prefabricated harbors were not completely finished, for one and a half million tons of equipment had to be convoyed across the Channel by 150 tugs. True, most of the massive Phoenix caissons had reached their resting places, but the long pier roadways needed calmer weather and seas in order to be towed. Some of the sections had been taken across in the adverse water of the first fortnight but it had required all the efforts and skill of the tugs to keep the roadways afloat for the ninety-mile trip.

Then a temporary improvement in the weather during the night of June 17-18 raised false hopes of possibly getting across the rest of the many lengths of pier roadway remaining in English ports just waiting for such a break in the weather.The problem seemed solved for Admiral Tennant, in charge of the operation, when the next evening, June 18, was so calm that he could follow a ripple all the way to the horizon. Back in Britain, Tennant's staff took immediate advantage of the weather to send twenty-two tows of roadway on their way for the French coast from the Solent. The meteorological report could not have been more favorable. The barometer was high, and the wind was westerly at force 3, indicating a gentle June breeze. After only a few hours the tows reached the Piccadilly zone without incident. All seemed set for a quiet crossing.

Then it happened: a sudden, sweeping change.

D+13, at 0800. The barometer fell, the wind rose—from force 3, to 5, to 8. Gale force without a warning. And not only a gale, but the worst northeaster in forty years—a couple of days short of midsummer. Halfway across the Channel, the twenty-two tows of pier roadways and Phoenix units met the maelstrom utterly unprepared. The gale gushed down from the North Sea and diagonally across the Channel, blowing into the invasion beaches, creating huge rollers that caught the unseaworthy, unprotected tows and hammered them heavily, until they had no chance of survival. The men on the tugs fought for their charges every inch and minute, but one by one they broke up and snapped their tows. Wild scenes ensued as loose roadways were seized in the grip of the gale, to be dashed finally against some strange French shore or driven to the bottom. Freshening each hour, the storm reached full gale force, until by the end of the day only one of the twenty-two tows still survived to reach France.

At the beachheads the storm's effect was just as devastating. All unloading stopped, and larger vessels in the invasion area struggled to sea to escape being driven ashore. Inside the two harbors the high spring tides made matters worse, for the water was deeper than usual. But despite this, some five hundred smaller craft crawled under the lee of the blockships to try and ride out the storm. Here they hung on desperately as the waters swirled round the half-hidden blockships. Somehow many survived, although hundreds of other vessels in the invasion fleet were picked up and hurled ashore or capsized.

The tide rose over the main deck of the *Durban* and low quarter-deck of the *Sumatra*. But the *Courbet* gave welcome protection to a crowd of craft cowering behind her, and not even this gale could damage her Cross of Lorraine, streaming straight out in the wind.

Sixteen blockships and twenty-four Phoenix had been planted at Arromanches, the Mulberry B harbor. Now as water and wind lashed at these hour after hour, four of the Phoenixes actually disintegrated. Day came again and still the gale howled. A littered tangle of steel marked high water. Piece by piece, more of the Phoenixes started to crack. And finally the Bombardon breakwaters also gave up, torn free by the force of waves 15 feet high and 300 feet long. These outer bastions had stood up to the sea for thirty hours: a day and a quarter. But now they broke and drifted ashore.

At 0400 on the second morning, the barometer rose fractionally, but the wind went on—and on. It was indeed fortunate for the Allies that the Calvados Reef did a lot to quell the storm's fury in Mulberry B.

But at Mulberry A the disaster was almost complete. The St. Laurent harbor had been built very quickly but in deeper and more exposed water than that at Arromanches. Breaches in the breakwater came quickly. And the Americans had planted their blockships so that there were still great gaps in the middle. These were meant to make communication with the shore easy for their assault craft, but in fact they let in the full force of the gale. Blockships broke up in a frenzy of rending steel. The old battleship *Centurian* was one of these. And as the raging sea scoured away the shifting sand in the harbor, others of the blockships settled deeper on the bottom and thus let in more of the storm.

Head on to the northeaster, the Mulberry A Phoenix caisson breakwater cracked, crumbled, and finally disintegrated. Far out, too, the 200 feet of semisubmerged floating steel Bombardon bastions were ripped loose to be flung and flailed against the shattering Phoenix units.

Through the breaches the sea struck at the roadways and piers, so that they were soon starting to submerge. The harbor had been crammed with craft when the storm struck and now many broke free and drifted down to the half-submerged Whale piers, battering at their floating supports till they sank. And all the while, craft, equipment, piers, and steel roadway were driven relentlessly inshore, till along the edge of the sea lay a grotesque pile of wreckage. And still the wind went on howling.

So Mulberry A had to be abandoned and as much of its equipment as possible salvaged and transferred to Arromanches, where a remarkable harbor was developed during July.

The gale eased slowly on June 22 and by the next day the sea had subsided, and Admirals Ramsay and Tennant could survey the sad scenes of Arromanches and St. Laurent. Apart from the loss of the whole of Mulberry A, the most serious result was that some eight hundred craft of all types stood stranded, high and dry with no chance of being refloated until the next spring tides. Then quite remarkably six hundred of them went back into service repaired and refloated, followed by a further hundred a fortnight later. So seven-eighths of the casualties to craft were salvaged.

Yet to all this there is a really remarkable postscript. If General Eisenhower had postponed D-Day from June 6, the next possible dates would have been about June 17 or 18. And remember, it was on June 19 that the great gale and storm swept down on those bare beaches. What would have happened? The Allied armies might well have been stranded in France without sufficient supplies or reserves to fight their way inland—or to hold on to the beachhead. No one knows. But it could have changed the course of history.

Meanwhile history was being made as the storm dashed the American harbor—and hopes—at St. Laurent.

"Cherbourg must be held at any price." So spoke Hitler as the Americans raced to seal off the Cotentin peninsula and then swung north toward the port piercing line after line of German defenses until at last they reached a point only three miles from Cherbourg. Now at the height of the storm at sea, the Americans mounted a great assault on the ditches, wire and mines which were the port's last lines of defense. The Germans resisted bitterly, refusing to surrender when called on to do so on June 21, and three more days of fanatical fighting followed before the Americans could enter the port. Even then the harbor forts held out for yet another three days until the capture was completed on June 27. Now the Allies had a real port to replace the man-made one lost almost simultaneously.

While the mopping up still went on in Cherbourg, special naval frogmen were embarked from Falmouth for the French port. On June 27, the day of Cherbourg's surrender, they were anchored off Utah beach, where they got orders to hurry overland to the port.

The United States port authority had not been idle, for the frog-

230

men received confirmation from them of the presence of a new German mine, about which they had heard in London. Known to the sweeping service as Katy, it consisted of an explosive charge set in a concrete block surmounted by a tripod of steel tubing. These mines were lowered to the bottom of the harbor and long greenish snag lines which were almost impossible to detect floated from them. Once a vessel fouled these snag lines with its propellers and hauled it taut, it fired the charge.

Soon their efforts met with success. Able Seaman M. H. Woods dived to look for mines in a large dry dock which could not be pumped dry because the machinery had been destroyed. Woods was using a buoyant rubber float attached to him to indicate his position, and soon his two maintenance men in a dinghy saw this float suddenly stop. They rowed over at once and gave one pull on the line to ask Woods if he was all right—but got no reply signal. After two more attempts they assumed he had blacked out and started to haul him up. But even with their officer's help the two sailors could not move him, until to their amazement Woods suddenly surfaced quite a long way off. He had found a K mine, and to be sure of being able to find it again had cast off his float line and secured it to the mine. So the men had been trying to haul up a live mine weighing almost a ton. Lieutenant Commander Harries dived on the mine, confirmed that it was a K wired for electrical control from the shore and rendered it safe.

So Cherbourg's channels, docks and harbor were cleared for Allied traffic—and one of the most invaluable and imaginative projects of all the amazing achievements associated with D-Day went into operation.

PLUTO—Pipe Line Under The Ocean.

Now that they were driving the Nazis back, the Allied divisions had to have fuel for their tanks, trucks, jeeps, motorbikes, and their myriad other vehicles.

As early as 1942 a 1,000-mile network of pipelines was being built in Britain to carry gasoline landed at the safer western ports to London and the south and east coasts. From Avonmouth on the Bristol Channel and Stanlow on the Mersey, it flowed south and east to Thames Haven and the Isle of Grain.

But if gasoline could be piped across England, why couldn't it be piped on to France? So the back-room boys set about it and eventually evolved a special three-inch-diameter pipe. The next step was to build the pumping stations on the Isle of Wight and at Dungeness. This latter was intended for use later in the war to take fuel across to Calais, but the first link would be from the Isle of Wight to Cherbourg.

British Royal Engineers and Royal Army Service Corps troops trained to work the pumps and the stations were carefully camouflaged to keep the plan secret. The next need was for special ships big enough to carry two-mile coils of this piping. After months of preparation, the first 70-mile span to Cherbourg started. At a steady five knots the vessel advanced, the pipeline unwinding from a roller at the stern of the ship. Each two miles, another vessel with another length of heavy coils would take over. Seventy miles and then at last the final link as a barge came out to join the pipeline to the beaches. Three more of these cross-Channel links were added later to make four pipelines under the ocean. It was just one more miracle to add to the story of D-Day.

Twenty-two

HITLER'S final strike against the invasion coast came secretly, silently. It was his last throw, and he must have known that if it failed the war would eventually be lost.

His first secret weapon at the very beginning of the war had been the magnetic mine. His latest one was the oyster mine. And to tell this strange story, we must go right back to the days of Dunkirk. By 1940, thanks to the courage of Commander John Ouvry and others, the British had found the answer to the magnetic mine. Soon they were also able to take countermeasures against the acoustic mine. And all the while, throughout the first four years of the war the British themselves were busily developing an oyster —and trying to discover a satisfactory way of sweeping such a mine. For it was one thing to be able to lay a mine; quite another if an antidote were not known, for an enemy could copy it.

Actually, both the Germans and the British produced examples of this amazing weapon which worked on the principle that the wave-trough of a ship causes water pressure on the sea bed to drop. A unit was thus evolved to react to just such a change—and fire a mine as the ship passed overhead. But despite every effort conceivable, no antidote could be found. It defied sweeping, so that as soon as one side used it, the other could conceivably retrieve one, copy it, and the idea would boomerang. Yet only in desperate circumstances would a naval commander consider using such a device while there was still no known countermeasure.

While the British oyster program progressed, the Germans were also working on one, too, *completely unknown to the British.*

The Germans' efforts all stemmed from an idea of their Lieutenant Commander Fett who got hold of a constructional survey of

233

the English canal system in which he noticed that as a ship pushed an extended wave ahead of her, this trough caused a variation in water pressure beneath her. The fact soon suggested an application to triggering a sea mine, but Fett's brain child met with little enthusiasm until the war was in its most desperate period. Then the Germans thought it might be wise to explore every possible secret weapon, and so took the idea a step further in deciding to combine it with some additional firing "trigger"—just to make it more impossible to sweep. And in their own peculiar fashion two oysters were developed along independent lines, one by the German air force, the other by the navy.

The net result was that utterly unknown to the Allies the Luftwaffe was producing "acoustic oysters" relying on water pressure plus the trigger of the sound of a ship, while the German navy gave birth to "magnetic oysters" combining the change in water pressure with the effect of a ship's magnetic field to fire the mine.

By the end of 1943, both branches of the German forces had workable versions of the oyster—and nothing to counteract them. The mines were put into production and actually assembled, but laying was strictly prohibited unless a national emergency occurred.

Realizing that invasion was likely soon, Hitler ordered 2,000 oysters sent to France to be laid the moment an assault was reported. A further 2,000 were held in readiness first in Germany and Norway, and then later in Holland. So great was the secrecy surrounding them that no one—not even senior officers in the Luftwaffe who would be called on to supervise laying them—was instructed in their nature or preparation until April, 1944. They were to be laid only on receipt of an explicit personal command from the Fuehrer.

April turned to May, and at the beginning of that month, an amazing stroke of luck happened—the first of two which might have made all the difference to the success of the invasion.

Goering suddenly ordered all oysters returned to Germany. This took time, and the whole operation was not completed until the first few days of June, when the last batch reached Magdeburg —only a day or two before the invasion!

Goering's unfortunate decision was made for two or three

reasons. He knew that the ersatz rubber bag, which was the vital pressure part of the mine, would have a fairly short life and was due to be superseded by another one made of a better material. Actually, the original rubber would have lasted long enough in the water for the short-term shock purpose intended.

The decision was also influenced by German intelligence, which gave him a probable site for any Allied landings in the immediate future. The invasion was evidently expected on the west coast of France opposite the Atlantic. Oysters were considered of less use in these deep, exposed waters of the Biscay seaboard; the effect of the swell would compromise them, and the depth was too great for them to have full effect. In addition, the order was sent to prevent the mines stored at Le Mans from being overrun before they could be used. Thus as long as the Germans remained ignorant of where the assault would come, they could not lay their oysters with the devastating effect they hoped. They just had to wait and see.

So it was that the unsweepable oysters were far away in the Fatherland and more or less unavailable as the thousands of vulnerable warships and landing craft prepared for the great assault. But the Nazi High Command felt that if the oysters could be laid soon after an invasion and the seas kept calm, Allied ships could not survive and the supply lines would be broken.

Meanwhile, back in Britain, the Allies were wondering what to expect in the manner of enemy mines. The recent mine-laying raids in the extreme western Solent had revealed only that the Germans were still relying on advanced forms of acoustic circuits. The specimens recovered revealed nothing new about the mines to be met off Normandy. But to be ready to meet an emergency, H.M.S. *Vernon,* the Royal Navy's special antimine training vessel, briefed several officers to accompany the invasion and try to find fresh mines.

Then came D-Day. And at once the order to lay the oysters came through from the German High Command.

But during the first week of June the R.A.F. and the Americans had been blasting all lines of communication between Germany and France—and that meant Magdeburg and the advanced Ger-

235

man airfields from which the mine-laying planes operated. Thus precious days passed before the order could be implemented.

While the oysters were being hurried by road and rail—where lines remained—the Germans intensified mining and other sea activity as they recovered from the initial shock of D-Day. They immediately reinforced their E-boats in Le Havre and Cherbourg, and the first signs of their mine laying in the actual assault area came on June 9 when E-boats attempted to restrict the build-up of vital supplies by laying a mine barrier on the northern flank of the Western Task Force, the Royal Navy's route to the British invasion coasts. Most of these surface attempts were beaten off, but soon afterward the Luftwaffe began mine laying, too, and this proved very hard to prevent or mark accurately as the aircraft operated only at night and flew in too quickly and too low to be picked up by Allied radar, and thus avoided Allied night fighters.

It was about this time that the Germans managed to get the first of their oysters back from Magdeburg, and they were rushed into service at once.

Now was a vital period for both sides. The Allies were well established in Normandy, but they could not yet stand any interruption to their lines of supply. And these ran through waters highly susceptible to mining.

For the Germans, this was the now or never, make or break moment.

Suddenly Allied ships started to be sunk. Steaming through swept channels, one had its back broken by the deadly, devastating eruption of a German mine. Soon another one went, her bow pointing high to heaven before plunging into the grave of Seine Bay. The problem of sweeping noncontact ground mines became more and more worrisome, as the involved minesweeping paraphernalia was inevitably liable to foul other ships and craft. And if the minesweepers were tackling an acoustic mine, there was the added uncertainty of the distance from the sweeper that the mine might explode—thus creating a constant menace to neighboring ships moored in the bay. Sweeping an open sea was plain sailing, but finding and firing magnetic or acoustic mines lying on the sea bed right among the Allied ships proved dramatically difficult.

Day by day, ships were sunk and men died. D+10 ... D+11 ... D+12 ... the unexplained sinkings went on.

The Allied naval officers detailed to search for new enemy mines were beginning their task, as the bridgehead became more stable, but they could not be expected to retrieve mines dropped by air into several fathoms off the coast.

Then on D+14 at Luc, the Allies had some luck!

Just as long before in November, 1939, when the Luftwaffe deposited a magnetic mine in the mud at Shoeburyness, so history was repeated. On the night of June 19-20, German aircraft flew through the rising gale to lay their latest batch of mines in Seine Bay.

The sound of the planes sent Allied ack-ack guns into action, and between the dark night, the gale beginning to blow, and the heavy fire from the ground, one pilot lost his sense of direction and jettisoned his mines too soon. As they fell, Sublieutenant Young of the Royal Navy was one of the men sheltering below at Luc-sur-Mer. He heard a deafening burst as one mine came down not in the sea but on the town and exploded. Then a moment later there was a second, more muffled explosion.

Next morning, Young went to investigate and found a house flattened by the first mine, which was designed to explode on contact with the ground if dropped by mistake. But the second weapon lay with only the end blown off. Young recognized it as a mine at once and examined the outside of its rear end, which concealed all the mechanism. At first, it seemed to be a type he knew: there was the bulge concealing the photoelectric cells. These devilish devices had been built into many German mines to try to prevent the Allies stripping them to see what was inside. The arrangement was that as soon as someone unscrewed the rear door of the mine and let in a scrap of light, the photoelectric cells made a contact and fired the whole mine, killing anyone within range. Yes, he knew all about these.

Then suddenly he spotted something he did *not* understand: an extra fitting on this rear end. It was only a slight variation, but any little addition might be significant.

Young spoke to his senior officer, and they had it transferred to

237

a temporary advance airstrip, where a Spitfire flew it across to Thorney Island, the nearest airfield to Portsmouth, where men of H.M.S. *Vernon* were waiting to have a look at it.

Meanwhile as the gale blew itself out on the Far Shore, Admiral Ramsay was really worried by the mine menace and the hopelessness of not being able to do anything. Was it just that sweeping could not be carried out efficiently in the cramped conditions over there? Or was there something else they didn't know? Certainly casualties to Allied ships due to enemy mines were becoming serious. Partly, he knew, this was due to the ripening of mines laid earlier and not exploded by Allied minesweepers, as at the time, the mines were passive—and so proof against sweeping. Then after a time—a delay clock would operate, the mines became active again and fired the first ship which actuated them. Thus there had to be frequent sweeps to overcome these mines.

The new lays were also worrying him, but there was still not much to be done until a definite diagnosis could be made as to their character. It was useless trying to cure something you weren't sure about.

Over at Thorney Island, the mine was unloaded carefully from the plane: a shorn-off relic of the dark cylindrical shape it was before being blown in half.

"Look at that." Someone pointed to the external rubber fitting.

"My God, it looks like an oyster!"

Still they could not be sure until they stripped the rear end and analyzed the complicated contents. So the scientists immediately started the procedure which even fifteen years later is still secret. They had to try and find out what made the mine work without losing their lives in the process.

They trepanned holes in the rear end by a remote-control trepanning machine, lying concealed at a respectable distance, and only when it was dark did they risk completing the openings and disconnecting any surviving leads. Now it was safe.

They started examining the complicated mechanism and soon found a microphone indicating an acoustic circuit. Then they examined the rubber pressure unit.

"It's an oyster, all right. No doubt about it."

Working furiously they checked the circuits to make sure, and then as soon as they were sure, a phone call to the Admiralty reported their discovery: an acoustic oyster which required both the sound of a ship's engines plus the altered water pressure caused by the vessel passing overhead to detonate it.

No solution was known, but at least countermeasures could be tried. It was better than sitting waiting for something to happen.

.Within hours of the report's arrival at the Admiralty, all ships in invasion waters were ordered to reduce speed to a minimum when within the actual assault area. This rule was strictly enforced, and although only an expedient, it cut down the casualties to a fraction of their former level.

Then the minesweepers went into action again. But although no foolproof method had been found to deal with the acoustic and magnetic oysters now being laid, it soon became obvious that neither was enjoying as much success as had been anticipated. Why? Because the Allies enjoyed a second bit of luck. The first had been when the oysters were not ready for D-Day. Now the weather, which had so seriously hurt the Allies, came to their help instead. The Luftwaffe had counted on calm, good weather in the period immediately following the invasion. Instead the seas were high and the swell triggered the pressure, or oyster side of the firing circuits without any ship passing overhead. This left the sweepers only the other half of the circuit to actuate, which they could do acoustically—so that the mines were often all sweepable. Plain acoustic sweepers with their vibrating hammers thus defeated the acoustic oysters.

The magnetic oysters, too, were often spoiled by the swell, which made the pressure side actuate prematurely. This would have still been all right if the ships had continued coming in fast, but the reduced speed also reduced the magnetic field they created —if their de-gaussing did not do the trick—so that they failed to fire the magnetic oysters.

By July 3 it was estimated that including spontaneous explosions caused by the elements, nearly 500 mines had been accounted for by the sweepers, and although the threat lingered on, the period of greatest danger was over. By the end of July, more than 2,000